RENEWAL

Indigenous Perspectives on Land-Based Education
In and Beyond the Classroom

Edited by Christine M'Lot and Katya Adamov Ferguson

PORTAGE &
MAIN PRESS

Portage & Main Press gratefully acknowledges the financial support of the Government of
Canada as well as the Province of Manitoba through the Department of Sport, Culture, Heritage
and Tourism and the Manitoba Book Publishing Tax Credit for our publishing activities.

Funded by the Government of Canada
Financé par le gouvernement du Canada | Canadä

Printed and bound in Canada by Friesens.
Design by Jennifer Lum
Cover art by Reanna McKay (Merasty)
Land-based education consultant and reviewer: Dr. Brian Rice

Library and Archives Canada Cataloguing in Publication
Title: Renewal : Indigenous perspectives on land-based education in and
beyond the classroom / edited by Christine M'Lot and Katya Adamov Ferguson.
Other titles: Renewal (2025) Names: M'Lot, Christine (Educator), editor. | Ferguson, Katya, editor.
Series: Footbridge series. Description: Series statement: Footbridge series ; 2
Identifiers: Canadiana (print) 20250157691 | Canadiana (ebook) 20250157713
ISBN 9781774921678 (softcover) | ISBN 9781774921685 (EPUB) | ISBN 9781774921692 (PDF)
Subjects: LCSH: Human ecology—Study and teaching—Canada.
LCSH: Traditional ecological knowledge—Canada. | LCSH: Environmental justice—
Study and teaching—Canada. | LCSH: Culturally relevant pedagogy—Canada.
LCSH: Indigenous peoples—Education—Canada. | LCGFT: Instructional and educational works.
Classification: LCC GF28.C3 R46 2025 | DDC 304.2089/97071—dc23

28 27 26 25   1 2 3 4 5

This book is printed on FSC®-certified paper made with 30% post-consumer waste using alcohol-free
blanket wash. It was printed in Canada by Friesens. With plants powered by wind and hydroelectricity,
the company is 100% employee-owned and is committed to minimizing its ecological footprint.

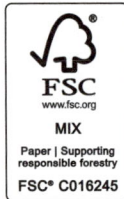

FSC
www.fsc.org
MIX
Paper | Supporting
responsible forestry
FSC® C016245

ENVIRONMENTAL BENEFITS STATEMENT
Portage & Main Press saved the following resources
by printing the pages of this book on chlorine free
paper made with 30% post-consumer waste.

TREES	WATER	ENERGY	SOLID WASTE	GREENHOUSE GASES
19 FULLY GROWN	1,600 GALLONS	8 MILLION BTUs	60 POUNDS	8,300 POUNDS

Environmental impact estimates were made using the Environmental Paper Network
Paper Calculator 4.0. For more information visit www.papercalculator.org

PORTAGE &
MAIN PRESS
www.portageandmainpress.com
Winnipeg, Manitoba
Treaty 1 Territory and homeland of the Métis Nation

*I would like to dedicate this volume to
those who've generously shared their wisdom, knowledge,
and experiences, and whose words fill these pages.*
—CM

*To my dad, who during his time on this Earth
taught me to respect the profound interactions
and relationships between living beings.*
—KAF

Contents

Acknowledgments

W E WOULD LIKE to thank *Renewal*'s land-based education consultant and reviewer, Dr. Brian Rice (Kanien'kehá:ka), for his support in this collaborative book project. He assisted in our search for contributors, advised us on topics in the field of land-based education, read our drafts, and consulted with us in varying capacities to ensure that we were on the right path.

Thank you to our editor, Caley Clements. We appreciated your keen eye for detail and your perspective of the bigger picture throughout the process of editing this land-centred collection. Your supportive suggestions have been important underpinnings in the building of this footbridge. We are grateful to Catherine Gerbasi and the amazing team at Portage & Main Press for this learning opportunity and for helping to make so many diverse topics accessible for learners of all ages.

Thanks to David A. Robertson, who, in the early phases of planning this book, suggested that to move forward in the face of the climate crisis, this text needed to focus on building better stewards of land who revere and respect land and water. He reminded us that kids often seem to "get it," but as adults, we need to learn how to "treat the land differently and draw strength from land and water."

Thank you to all the contributors who shared their unique perspectives of education on Indigenous lands. We know your words, images, songs, and poems will help transform practices in schools and far beyond. The opportunity to connect with many of you for conversations about your work and your commitment to education that prioritizes land helped to inform the Educator Connections sections. We are grateful to you for sharing your time, creativity, and wisdom, making this iteration of the Footbridge series possible.

Christine: I'd also like to acknowledge my 100-year-old kookum, Vina Swain, as some of my earliest memories as a child include the taste of the traditional medicines she put under my tongue when I was sick; my mother, Donna M'Lot, who ensured some of my first words were in our traditional language; David and Sherryl Blacksmith, who have welcomed me into ceremony; the late Elder Stella Blackbird, who shared teachings and wisdom at Medicine Eagle Camp; and Shirli Ewanchuk, who has invited me into her home for ceremony. Miigwetch for being generous with your teachings.

Katya: I am grateful to continue to learn from Indigenous leaders who have expertise and profound knowledge in this area. I want to acknowledge that the land-based work of Indigenous communities has never stopped. So much work has been done to preserve the land and this knowledge, and visionary educational teams are actively undertaking renewal efforts here in Winnipeg. I hope this important sustainability work continues to receive the substantial funding and prioritization it deserves.

Introduction

CHRISTINE M'LOT (she/her/hers) is an Anishinaabe educator and curriculum developer from Winnipeg, Manitoba. She currently teaches high school at the University of Winnipeg Collegiate and is the associate publisher at Portage & Main Press. To learn more about her past and current education projects, visit www.christinemlot.com.

KATYA ADAMOV FERGUSON (she/her/hers) is a settler educator and artist of Ukrainian and Russian ancestry from Winnipeg, Manitoba. Katya is also an arts-based researcher engaging with creative and critical methods to support place-based inquiries and deeper understandings of land-based issues. She is committed to creating partnerships and supporting Indigenous resurgence.

———

LAND-BASED EDUCATION is education *on* the land, *about* the land, and *from* the land. It is not simply "taking the classroom outside," although that may be one aspect of it. Land-based education relies on the *land as the teacher* and encompasses education pertaining to the sky, waters, land, and all of Earth's inhabitants. Land-based education reflects Indigenous philosophies and methods of education that are connected to specific places and rooted in history, language, and culture, as Indigenous nations have lived on the land, learned from the land, changed the land, adapted to the land, and acted as stewards of the land since time immemorial. Land-based education is interdisciplinary, fusing the sciences, social studies, mathematics, physical and health education, geography, global issues, and more. It is experiential and inclusive of all learners.

There are many reasons why you may have decided to learn more about land-based education. Perhaps your current teaching context feels hollow, as though it is more about school and schooling than life and living. Maybe you have seen how a hidden curriculum leaves students with a limited perspective of the history of the land where they live or positions land only as a resource to be extracted. Perhaps your most memorable and authentic learning experiences were on land and water, amongst animals and the natural world, and you want to share this with students. You may have seen first-hand how learning *on*, *about*, and *from* the land supports healing and well-being. Perhaps you are awakening to the fact that embracing Indigenous knowledge is essential to combatting the climate crisis and moving toward a more sustainable way of living. Or maybe you are here because the education department in your region has added Indigenous knowledges to the curriculum and you want to learn to integrate this into your teaching in a good way. Regardless of the reason you've chosen this book, *Renewal* will give you plenty to think about and offer concrete ways to bring this knowledge into your learning space.

The term *renewal* can be defined as the process of re-establishing or replenishing relationships, which may include connections between humans and non-human or more-than-human elements.[1] It acknowledges a response to the interruption of colonial schooling that aimed to distance peoples from land and from teachings and languages connected to land and community. To us, renewal is also about renewing our practices and priorities in relation to land-based education, while acknowledging that the field of land education is not new. The word *renewal* acknowledges the strengths of the past while expressing great hope for the future; both perspectives are needed to achieve a wholistic balance within and beyond the classroom.[2] We hope that reading these pages will help you establish, re-establish, or replenish your connection to land-based education.

---

1   Various terms are used to describe natural elements that are not human, including non-human, more than human, and beyond human. They remind us that humans are not the most important living entities on Earth and reveal interspecies connections among those dwelling on this planet. They can also remind us of spiritual aspects of the natural world.

2   We prefer *wholistic* to *holistic*, which indicates "'whole' as in...complete, balanced, and circular," as described in Kathy Absolon, "Indigenous Wholistic Theory: A Knowledge Set for Practice," *First Peoples Child & Family Review* 5, no. 2 (2010): 75.

The overarching goal of *Renewal* is to support educators in integrating Indigenous land-based pedagogies in both the classroom and outdoor settings. As we, an experienced Indigenous educator and non-Indigenous educator, are not experts in land-based education, we walk alongside you in this learning. The contributors whose works are featured in this book are Indigenous leaders—thinkers, artists, creatives, and activists—who guide us through many ways of knowing, being, and doing in relation to the land. They model how to live as relatives to the land, through a variety of actions: walking, painting, singing, researching, photographing, travelling, writing, performing, protesting, planning, healing, listening, reimagining. They invite us to ask what this can mean for us in the places where we live and learn. Though their work is grounded in the present, it acts as a bridge to many past generations who remained connected to the land, resisting the destructive colonial practices that actively sought to destroy these connections. In this collaborative project, we treat each piece as a "living text" that acts as a springboard for engaging with Indigenous voices and pedagogies. At the core of this text, we seek to foster a profound awareness and appreciation of our intrinsic connection to the land, emphasizing its vital role in shaping culture, identity, and well-being.

What Is Indigenous Education? What Is Land-Based Education?

Land-based education is a fundamental aspect of Indigenous education. Indigenous education is a multifaceted concept rooted in the rich histories, teachings, and traditions of Indigenous nations. The term *Indigenous* refers to First Nations, Métis, and Inuit communities and peoples in Canada collectively. It is important to recognize that there are similarities and differences among and between Indigenous groups. At its core, Indigenous education acknowledges the unique stories and deep wisdom possessed by every Indigenous nation, recognizing that each has its own sacred teachings passed down through generations. The contributors to *Renewal* reflect a variety of Indigenous nations, teachings, and perspectives, grounding the text in specific communities and lands.

For non-Indigenous educators, engaging with Indigenous education may bring up feelings of discomfort or anxiety about "getting it wrong." But by working patiently and with a good heart, you can learn alongside your students, acting as a facilitator of knowledge rather than an expert. As you engage with the texts and classroom materials in *Renewal*, be mindful to avoid mimicking Indigenous cultural practices, ceremonies, and artwork. If you are wondering about the appropriateness of any activity, we encourage you to consult Elders, Knowledge Keepers, and members of local Indigenous communities whenever possible. We have tried to provide helpful learning extensions but acknowledge that opinions on what may or may not be suitable in certain settings differ. Asking questions is part of the learning, and we hope you will seek out and continue learning from Indigenous leaders in land-based practices.

Indigenous educational approaches are wholistic and inclusive, welcoming all individuals and making space for them. Indigenous intelligences encompass a wide range of abilities, including the capacity to learn from observations, absorb teachings and oral history through storytelling, express oneself orally, and have intuitive insights.[3] Additionally, Indigenous education emphasizes getting involved in one's community. Many of the supporting materials in the Classroom Connections sections throughout *Renewal* are centred on these principles, encouraging readers to learn through observation, listening, and discussion and to take action in response.

A fundamental aspect of Indigenous education is its deep connections to the land. It encompasses content and processes that are land-based, emphasizing an intimate relationship with the land—being of the land, being on the land, and understanding the land. Traditionally, living harmoniously with the land required cross-disciplinary expertise in geology, geography, biology, physics, mathematics, and engineering, and this still rings true today. The contributors to this book have a wide range of experience and use different modes of expression to share their understandings, demonstrating how land-based learning takes many forms.

---

3   Red Rising, "Red Rising Education Resource Video," YouTube, 13:34, www.youtube.com /watch?v=G4bcSaumWfo&t=198s, at 40 seconds.

Indigenous ways of knowing, being, doing, and becoming are the pillars of land-based education, emphasizing a symbiotic relationship with the environment. Central to this is the understanding that land is not merely a physical locale or property to acquire, but a living entity woven into the foundation of Indigenous worldviews encompassing the land, water, sky, and animals. Throughout this book, we use the term *land* broadly, and with utmost respect for its complex meanings. When we talk about land, we mean land and water. Human beings are and always will be connected in our physical form to both. In his essay on page 194, Nehinuw scholar Réal Carrière helps us think about the meaning of *land*: "The 'land' of 'land-based' is more than a place. The land is spiritual. The land is physical."

By reframing land-based education in this way, educators can tap into a wide breadth of knowledge and wisdom beyond the four walls of the school. The land is a dynamic classroom where lessons can unfold organically through observation, reflection, conversation, and participation. By centring Indigenous perspectives, educators can create inclusive learning environments that honour diverse ways of knowing and being, fostering a sense of belonging and empowerment among students. Through this reframing, educational opportunities expand to encompass not only academic growth but also personal and cultural enrichment, nurturing students' wholistic development and fostering a deeper understanding of their place within the broader web of existence. The contributors featured in *Renewal* help us think about what land-based education was, what it is for now, and how it may continue to change in the future.[4]

---

4 We acknowledge that discourses around land-based education are changing and shifting, and we have noticed that at times it is being referred to as *land education*. Reverence and respect for the land can also be emphasized by capitalizing this term (i.e., Land).

Why Is Land-Based Education Important for All Learners?

There is no substitute for the profound experience of learning and being on the land. Directly engaging students with the land and her stories and lessons has a transformative effect that transcends conventional classroom education. Schools today are integrating land-based pedagogies in various ways, from outdoor education initiatives to place-based inquiries, to Indigenous Traditional Ecological Knowledge, to designing their own relevant local curricula. Each method carries its own distinct worldview and objectives, shaped by cultural, regional, and community-specific needs and nuances. *Renewal* encourages educators not to be constrained or limited by their location, as land-based learning can take place anywhere, including in urban areas.

Renowned Métis visual artist Christi Belcourt powerfully states that

> the only education that our children need is from the land. Educators and academics, you can do more than you realize. You must have the courage to disrupt the system for the sake of our children and our grandchildren. You must have the courage to join with each other to turn the system on its head. You must rebuild so schools cease being institutions, and return to their natural state of bringing children to the land.[5]

We believe Belcourt's assertions can apply to all students. While connecting to land and water is natural, land-based education can be seen as revolutionary in that it goes against current norms. Connecting to land and water will prompt educators to reflect on new learning priorities alongside the consequences of the colonial past and present. Embedding Indigenous land-based knowledge within current education systems is an important step toward reconciliation.

---

5   Christi Belcourt, "Chapter 7: The Revolution Has Begun," in *Toward What Justice? Describing Diverse Dreams of Justice in Education*, ed. Eve Tuck and K. Wayne Yang (Taylor & Francis, 2018), 120.

Land-based education focuses energy on seeing the places where we live through a new lens and developing renewed relationships with land that demonstrate a commitment to action. Throughout *Renewal*, you will notice the contributors' physical, emotional, and spiritual connections to land, water, animals, and air. They nudge us to become aware of and unlearn the anthropocentric notion that humans are more important than other animals and living things.

In addition, because land-based learning is wholistic and engages multiple aspects of ourselves, it can support student and educator well-being. An emerging consideration is the intersection of land-based education and provisions for neurodiversity and various learning needs among students, highlighting the inclusivity and adaptability of these Indigenous pedagogies. On a practical level, in our own teaching experiences we have witnessed how connecting to the land can support students in ways that a traditional classroom setting cannot. Students who have challenges communicating, regulating, and participating in the regular classroom setting become leaders when learning shifts to an outdoor environment. Connecting to nature in small and intentional ways may shift perspectives about how children learn and who is able to achieve success. Reconnecting to land and water can help us all relate and regulate.

Why *Renewal*?

Land-based education is a way of learning and taking action that can advance truth and reconciliation. It does so by grounding learning in relation to historic removals from land and relationships between land and language. It is important for educators to address historic injustices and build meaningful connections to specific nations and territories that are centred around understanding and respect. In his essay on page 184, Kanien'kehá:ka scholar Dan Henhawk calls for a renewal of attention to Indigenous ways of knowing, being, and doing; he notes, "It's not that Indigenous knowledges are lost, but rather that human beings have stopped listening."

Renewal's contributors guide us in understanding issues surrounding land, including how land dispossession has been used to control and dishonour Indigenous Peoples. Their reflections expose the consequences of ongoing injustices, environmental racism, and consumerism. As Valérie Courtois (Innu), a leader in Indigenous-led conservation and stewardship, states, "One of the worst impacts of colonialism was to remove Indigenous Peoples from our landscapes—the places where we find our strength, our identity, and our place in this world. Taking us away from our lands—through residential school and other forced removals—has been profoundly traumatic. But the reverse is also true: reconnecting with the land heals us."[6] The contributors balance the difficult historical truths and contemporary challenges with empowering and healing aspects of connection and reconnection to land. Their personal perspectives establish paths forward.

The Truth and Reconciliation Commission of Canada (TRC) states: "Reconciliation must support Aboriginal peoples as they heal from the destructive legacies of colonization that have wreaked such havoc in their lives. But it must do even more. Reconciliation must inspire Aboriginal and non-Aboriginal peoples to transform Canadian society so that our children and grandchildren can live together in dignity, peace, and prosperity on these lands we now share."[7]

The TRC emphasized this in Call to Action 45, which addresses land and water rights.[8] In part, it calls upon the government of Canada to:

i. Repudiate concepts used to justify European sovereignty over Indigenous lands and peoples, such as the Doctrine of Discovery and *terra nullius*.

ii. Adopt and implement the United Nations Declaration on the Rights of Indigenous Peoples as the framework for reconciliation.

---

6   Valérie Courtois, "Reconciliation Happens on the Land," Indigenous Leadership Initiative, September 29, 2021, www.ilinationhood.ca/blog/reconciliationontheland.

7   Truth and Reconciliation Commission of Canada, *Canada's Residential Schools: Reconciliation, The Final Report of the Truth and Reconciliation Commission of Canada*, Volume 6 (McGill-Queen's University Press, 2015), 4.

8   Truth and Reconciliation Commission of Canada, *Truth and Reconciliation Commission of Canada: Calls to Action* (2015), ehprnh2mwo3.exactdn.com/wp-content/uploads/2021/01/Calls_to_Action_English2.pdf.

This Call to Action underscores the need for a deeper understanding of and respect for Indigenous knowledge and traditions. The concept of *terra nullius* (or nobody's land) incorrectly viewed the land as empty and uninhabited. This led to land grabs that prioritized the settler quest for property over Indigenous ways of knowing and being that were *already here* and were intrinsically connected to the land. By incorporating Indigenous knowledge systems, languages, and traditions into land-based education, educators can empower students to challenge dominant narratives and advocate for Indigenous rights and sovereignty.

The idea of an international standard on Indigenous Peoples' rights grew from several grassroots Indigenous movements in North America, as well as the Civil Rights Movement in the United States.[9] The United Nations Declaration on the Rights of Indigenous Peoples was adopted by the United Nations General Assembly in 2007. It outlines the rights of Indigenous Peoples around the world, including those related to cultural preservation, the land, and self-determination.

Today, as we stand on the precipice of a looming climate catastrophe, it is paramount that we fundamentally shift our perspectives and behaviours toward the land, water, and environmental sustainability. This necessitates acknowledging settler colonialism and its pervasive impact. By confronting historical and ongoing injustices, we can work toward a more ecologically conscious future.

The contemporary Land Back movement highlights the urgent need to restore traditional lands and rights to Indigenous communities. This movement emphasizes the fundamental connection between Indigenous Peoples and ancestral territories, advocating for the return of land that has been unjustly taken through colonization, dispossession, and government policies. The Land Back movement in Canada is not attributed to a single individual or group but represents a collective effort by Indigenous Peoples and communities. The idea of Land Back is integral to *Renewal,* providing students and educators with opportunities to think about their understandings

---

9   Sheryl Lightfoot, "The Road to Reconciliation Starts With the UN Declaration on the Rights of Indigenous Peoples," The Conversation, September 12, 2019, theconversation.com/the-road-to-reconciliation-starts-with-the-un-declaration-on-the-rights-of-indigenous-peoples-122305.

of settler colonialism, and to consider what actions can be taken to support Indigenous sovereignty and stewardship over ancestral lands.[10]

Treaty relationships, which have significant historical and legal importance, play a crucial role in these discussions. Beyond their importance as legal agreements, treaties also embody promises and commitments made between Indigenous nations and colonial authorities. They often include provisions for land rights, resource sharing, and the protection of Indigenous sovereignty. Recognizing and respecting these treaty relationships is an essential step toward achieving reconciliation and justice in the ongoing dialogue about land and water. Throughout *Renewal*, we encourage you to learn more about relationships to land as outlined in treaties and to critically consider the extent to which these documented partnerships and rights have been upheld and honoured.

Land and language are intricately connected and are a steady stream flowing through this book that gives insight into worldviews of Indigenous communities. A crucial element of land-based education is acknowledging Indigenous place names, which offer insights into the historical, cultural, and spiritual significance of a region. New understandings of land and water or other land-based terms can surface through learning Indigenous words.

Land and water also connect to contemporary issues that require urgent attention. Bodies of Indigenous women are buried in landfills. Unmarked graves of Indigenous children are found on the grounds of Indian residential schools and in burial grounds hidden beneath the pavement of our cities. Ongoing and unchecked poisoning of water sources continues on reserves. These haunting connections to the past are surfacing in public discussions with increasing frequency. Understanding these issues and connecting to land are part of acknowledging responsibility and taking important restorative steps as educators.

Sara Florence Davidson (Haida) reminds us that "in the past, the emphasis has been placed upon including Indigenous content (information *about* Indigenous Peoples) without necessarily considering who created the materials, thus the inclusion of Indigenous *content* was prioritized over the

---

10 For each text featured in this book, see the Connecting to Land Back section for specific links to the Land Back movement.

12

representation of Indigenous *perspectives*" (original emphasis).[11] In *Renewal*, we maintain a commitment to a diverse representation of Indigenous perspectives and a variety of ways of knowing, being, and doing to engage with physical, mental, emotional, and spiritual elements that connect us to land and water. While the editing team represents a collaborative effort between Indigenous and non-Indigenous teachers, the contributions themselves are representative of First Nations, Métis, and Inuit perspectives.

The contributors prompt us to think about land, exploring topics such as ancestral homelands and waterways, stolen lands and the long-lasting damage of colonialism, and ways of acting to ensure a healthy planet for future generations. Kanien'kehá:ka scholar Dan Henhawk prompts us to think deeply about how we can renew our relationship with land: "What would happen if we approached the world, and our own activities, with an understanding of our obligations as human beings to live in respectful relations with each other and with all our relations on the land, in the water, and throughout the cosmos?" (page 185).

The variety of nations represented here nudges us beyond our personal orientations and the lands and waters we may know best. The contributors' perspectives and voices encourage readers to think about common ground among diverging viewpoints and experiences. For settler educators, the contributors provide advice for how to become active participants in land-based education and be mindful about appropriation. While our roles and responsibilities may vary and we may take action in different ways and contexts, the voices heard here make us think about how we can look to the land as teacher. In response to the contributors' gifts, we offer practical and concrete ways to facilitate discussions around land-based topics, advice on land-based activities, and suggestions for how students can engage with these topics through inquiry learning. Both the texts and supporting materials provide guidance in renewing our relationships with land and ensuring this is done in a respectful way.

---

11   Sara Florence Davidson, "Evaluating Indigenous Education Resources for Classroom Use," *Teacher* [BC Teachers' Federation Magazine] 32, no. 5 (May/June 2020): 22, www.bctf.ca/docs/default -source/publications/publications-teacher-magazine/teacher-may-2020.pdf?sfvrsn=66291b19_0.

We extend readers an invitation to actively engage with *Renewal*'s content. We hope that this book serves as a platform for innovative thinking, and we encourage you to draw inspiration from the diverse texts and prompts to craft lesson plans that resonate with your unique perspective and teaching style. In doing so, you will not only deepen your understanding of Indigenous land-based education, but also cultivate the skills and insights necessary for imparting this knowledge to future generations.

Land-Based Education: How to Begin?

RECOMMENDED APPROACHES

- *Prioritize safety lessons.* Safety lessons should happen before any outdoor activities and as new situations and conditions arise. For example, if students will be going outside in the winter, they should first learn how to stay warm and recognize the signs of hypothermia.

- *Build and maintain Indigenous community partnerships.* This is an essential step in the full experience of land-based education. This may take time and patience; however, remember that this is *part* of the learning, not an obstacle to it. Find ways that you can give back to and support local Indigenous communities.

- *Involve Elders and Knowledge Keepers.* The involvement of Elders and Knowledge Keepers is an essential aspect of land-based education. Elders and Knowledge Keepers hold traditional knowledge and teachings and should be treated with the utmost respect. We encourage you to connect with your school, division, or board's Elder-in-residence, Indigenous Education Lead, or consultant, or to reach out to your local Friendship Centre or other local Indigenous organization to request an introduction to an Elder or Knowledge Keeper.

  It is important to note that some Indigenous Elders and Knowledge Keepers are more comfortable talking about their areas of expertise, rather than adhering to a specific topic and presentation structure. Ensure that Elders and Knowledge Keepers have all the information they need to make their visit a success; for example, that they know where to go on the day of the visit and where the washroom is located.

Elders and Knowledge Keepers should be generously compensated for their time and, when possible, in keeping with local protocols. It is important to inquire about the appropriate protocols and proper compensation when requesting an Elder's or Knowledge Keeper's services, and to have payment or other forms of compensation ready at the conclusion of their visit.

We encourage educators to stay in touch with their guests. Consider having students write thank-you letters after you have debriefed the visit together. Educators who want to make meaningful connections with Indigenous communities may also consider attending local Indigenous events to demonstrate their support and commitment to lifelong learning.

- *Prioritize Indigenous languages.* We can learn a lot about Indigenous ways of knowing, being, doing, and becoming from the Indigenous words for various natural elements.

- *Honour Indigenous protocols.* For example, Indigenous communities often have specific cultural protocols that are followed when planting, harvesting, hunting, and feasting. If you are doing any of these activities, it is best to ask and follow the lead of Indigenous community partners. This is especially true if you will be engaging in ceremony, which should be conducted only by an Indigenous Elder or Knowledge Keeper. It is important to remember that if a teaching is shared with you, it does not mean you have permission to share it with others.

- *Invite local Indigenous youth to be helpers and participants.* Ensure that you create a safe space for community members and offer various roles so that individuals can contribute meaningfully.

GETTING STARTED CHECKLIST

1. Determine your goals:
   - Why do you want to include land-based education in your curriculum?
   - How might the experience connect with curricular outcomes and understandings?

- Do you want this to be a one-time event or ongoing?
- What do you want students to learn from the experience?
- What skills, knowledge, and experiences are relevant?
- Where will the learning take place? Will it be close to or far from the school?
- When will the learning take place?
- Do your student learning goals align with the proposed time and place? For example, medicine picking with the support of a Knowledge Keeper may only be possible in certain places and at a specific time of year; in this case, the season in which the medicine is available and plentiful enough to be harvested is an important consideration.

2. Determine who will be involved:
   - Which community experts would be valuable co-facilitators? For example, there might be a traditional fisher, hunter, astrologer, hide tanner, language speaker, or other relevant Knowledge Keeper from one of the First Nations in your area who you might want to reach out to.[12]
   - What is the cultural protocol for asking community experts for assistance? If you don't know, it is appropriate to ask the individual or organization which protocols should be followed. For example, for many First Nations and Métis Knowledge Keepers in Manitoba, passing tobacco is an accepted protocol when asking for help, guidance, teachings, or collaboration in addition to monetary compensation for time, travel, and expertise.
   - Are there any students/youth that could act as helpers?
   - Are there any community organizations you can partner with? For example, to connect with a local First Nation, you can call the band office, school, or cultural centre.

---

12 See Herman J. Michell, *Land-Based Education: Embracing the Rhythms of the Earth From an Indigenous Perspective* (JCharlton Publishing, 2018), 32–33.

- How can you form reciprocal relationships with the individuals or community partners you've reached out to? For example, in addition to providing an honorarium, you might offer to assist community members with their projects (e.g., working in their garden during harvest time).

- How will you bridge connections with students' families? Think about how parents and guardians could be involved in the learning, provide support from behind the scenes, or actively participate by sharing their knowledge.

3. Determine what the experience will entail:
   - What will students be learning and doing? Consider why this learning is important.
   - How will Indigenous knowledges and worldviews be incorporated throughout?
   - How will Indigenous languages be incorporated throughout?

4. Determine what resources you already have and what you will need:
   - What outdoor learning spaces are available nearby?
   - What resources do you already have access to? (e.g., equipment, supplies, safety items)
   - What items do you need and how will you get them?

5. Determine logistical details:
   - Will you provide the Knowledge Keeper or Elder an honorarium payment utilizing proper protocol prior to the experience, or on the day of?
   - How will your students get to the site?
   - How will your community partners or individuals get to the site?
   - How much time will be spent outdoors?
   - Is there an indoor space nearby?
   - Are there indoor or outdoor washroom facilities available?

- What will you eat?
- How will food be stored safely?
- Are there students with medical concerns? Will they have access to their medication?
- Who can assist you if there is an emergency?
- Will you have to send permission forms home?
- Will you ask for parent/community volunteers?

6. Determine what safety education is needed:[13]
   - What are the safety concerns associated with the experience? What precautions do students need to learn about before engaging in the experience?
   - Who will teach the safety lessons? Consider discussing some specific scenarios in advance.
   - How will you know students are ready for the experience?

7. Determine how students will document their experiences and learning:
   - Will students take notes or pictures during the experience?
   - Will students have time to reflect on their experience during the day? After?
   - How can students share or synthesize what they've learned?
   - Will students showcase their learning to the class, school, or larger community?

8. Determine how you will invite reflection on the experience:
   - How will you reflect on how the experience went?
   - How will the community partners, members, and volunteers' reflections on the day be listened to?

---

13   See Michell, *Land-Based Education*, 32–33.

RECOMMENDED RESOURCES

Bell, Nicole, Kim Wheatley, and Bob Johnson. *The Ways of Knowing Guide: Earth's Teachings.* Toronto Zoo, 2012. www.torontozoo.com/pdfs/tic/ways-of-knowing.pdf.

Canadian Commission for UNESCO. "Land as Teacher: Understanding Indigenous Land-Based Education." June 21, 2021. en.ccunesco.ca/idealab/indigenous-land-based-education.

Cherpako, Danielle R. *Indigenous-Led, Land-Based Programming: Facilitating Connection to the Land and Within the Community.* Social Connectedness Fellowship Program, Samuel Centre for Social Connectedness, 2019. www.socialconnectedness.org/wp-content/uploads/2019/10/Indigenous-Led-Land-Based-Programming.pdf.

Indigenous Education: The National Centre for Collaboration. "Stories—Land-Based Learning." Accessed August 26, 2024. www.nccie.ca/nccie-stories/stories-land-based-learning/.

Learning the Land. "Welcome to Learning the Land." Accessed August 26, 2024. learningtheland.ca.

Manitoba First Nations Education Resource Centre. *Land-Based Education Support Document for Educators.* Manitoba First Nations Education Resource Centre, 2023. mfnerc.org/product/land-based-education-support-document-for-educators/.

Michell, Herman J. *Land-Based Education: Embracing the Rhythms of the Earth From an Indigenous Perspective.* JCharlton Publishing, 2018.

Tkaronto CIRCLE Lab. Land Education Dreambook. Accessed May 21, 2025. landeducationdreambook.com.

Personal Connections

Christine: I recently decided to apply for (and successfully obtained) my treaty status. Given recent events where people have falsely claimed to be Indigenous, I thought it was important to have proof of my identity. Previously, I never cared if the government recognized me as an "Indian," as I felt confident in my identity as an Indigenous person. Even though I was born and raised in the city, some of my earliest memories include going to the annual Swan Lake powwow and visiting my kookum, Vina Swain, who lived in the town of Swan Lake. I had the privilege of hearing our traditional language, Anishinaabemowin, spoken in familial settings and attending ceremony to receive my spirit name as a teenager. When the idea of a land and water textbook came up, I was excited and somewhat nervous because it prompted me to think about my own connection to, and even disconnection from, land and water. I thought being raised in an urban centre had stifled my connection, but through Dr. Tasha Beeds's contribution (page 100), I came to realize that "it doesn't matter where you are...every time you pray, you activate; every time you sing, you activate; every time you give offerings or tobacco, you activate; every time you lift Pipes and Water, lift pen to write and fingers to type, sweat and fast, or dance, you activate." This revelation that connection to land and water can happen even in the concrete jungle of the city is just one way that my thoughts about my own connection to land and water have evolved throughout the journey of editing this book. I'm excited for you to read the contributions and reflect on your own connection to land and water.

Katya: When I think about my connections to land and water, I think about past, present, and future all at once. When I think about land, I think of foraging for mushrooms and blueberries in Manitoba and around the lakes in Ontario with my beloved grandparents. When I think about water, I am reminded of my dad and his knowledge of fish and the boreal forest. I wish I could discuss this book project with him, as he would undoubtedly have had connections and insights to share. In a way, discussions of land and water help me sustain this spiritual relationship with my dad, who is no longer on this Earth. I am connected to places where my grandparents are from: villages near Chernivtsi, Berdyansk, Kharkiv, and other places in Ukraine, Russia, and Eastern Europe. I maintain connections to these places through dancing, singing, sacred arts practices, and spiritual traditions, and through sharing these and working to preserve them for my family. Then I'm reminded of how land is the source of ongoing violence in my own ancestral homelands. These perspectives of land continue to shift. Anti-racist settler scholar Sheelah McLean reminds me to stay grounded in the reality that my own family are uninvited guests, colonizers, settlers who benefitted from the systems designed to oppress Indigenous Peoples.[14] We craved ownership of land and were unaware of the impacts of our arrival. Now I try to undo and unlearn "myths of meritocracy" in my work as a teacher.[15]

Indigenous ways of knowing, being, and doing have fundamentally changed my paths as a mother and teacher. I value my time learning within schools such as Niji Mahkwa School, which prioritizes Indigenous cultural practices and ceremony. In my artistic practice, I have drawn upon Earth-based art to help me speak from the heart as a way of communicating tensions between Indigenous and settler perspectives, and actively bringing attention to issues that are consistently marginalized. There is a Haida teaching, shared by Sandra Styres, that continues to remind me of the importance of land and water, sitting within my being as a mother: "We do not inherit the land from our ancestors—we borrow it from our children."[16]

---

14 Sheelah McLean, "'We Built a Life From Nothing': White Settler Colonialism and the Myth of Meritocracy," *Our Schools/Our Selves*, Fall/Winter 2018, policyalternatives.ca/sites/default/files/uploads/publications/National%20Office/2017/12/McLean.pdf.

15 McLean, "'We Built a Life From Nothing.'"

16 Sandra Styres, "Literacies of Land: Decolonizing Narratives, Storying & Literature," in *Indigenous and Decolonizing Studies in Education: Mapping the Long View*, ed. Linda Tuhiwai Smith, Eve Tuck, and K. Wayne Yang (Routledge, 2019), 24–37.

How This Book Is Organized

THIS BOOK is organized into four parts: Knowing, Being, Doing, and Becoming. These part titles are drawn from an approach to learning that is common among many Indigenous Peoples. The four interconnected aspects overlap throughout the book, but are most strongly represented in each respective part.

Part One: Knowing highlights Indigenous ways of knowing, which encompass the diverse epistemologies or knowledge systems developed by Indigenous Peoples over millennia. This knowledge is rooted in extensive observations and experiences, and is recorded in oral traditions such as stories, songs, and place names. It is intergenerational, passed down from Elders to youth, and is deeply tied to the land, culture, and spiritual practices.

Part Two: Being focuses on Indigenous ways of being, which refer to the ontological or philosophical perspectives that guide how Indigenous Peoples understand and interact with the world and view their place in it. This includes understandings of nature, human existence, kinship, and sustainability.

Part Three: Doing connects to Indigenous ways of doing, which involve the practical application of Indigenous knowledge in daily life and cultural practices. This includes life-sustaining activities such as hunting, fishing, and harvesting. Indigenous ways of doing also include spiritual and cultural practices such as ceremonies, storytelling, and artistic expressions.

Part Four: Becoming explores Indigenous ways of becoming, which focus on the process of growth and lifelong personal and communal development. This process highlights the importance of lifelong learning, adaptation, and the transmission of knowledge through generations. It involves cultivating a sense of identity and highlights the importance of individual and community well-being.

The Footbridge Framework

The Footbridge Framework first introduced in *Resurgence* serves as a guide for both educators and students, facilitating a meaningful connection with Indigenous perspectives and texts. Within this framework, the Educator and Classroom Connections sections that accompany each text offer valuable steps that can be taken to begin to bridge the gap between classrooms and Indigenous worldviews. The Connecting to Land-Based Learning and Connecting to Land Back sections (which are new to *Renewal*) provide ideas that encourage students to actively engage with their natural surroundings and critically reflect on topics related to land removals, colonial land claims, and the restoration of relationships with land.

EDUCATOR CONNECTIONS

❶ Preparing to Set Out

- **Part Overviews:** Think about the part's ideas and themes in relation to Indigenous ways of knowing, being, doing, and becoming.
- **Contributor Biographies** and **Contributor Narratives and Expressions:** Focus on the contributor, their relationship to place, and their work.
- **Personal Connections** and **Educator Inquiry and Actions:** Reflect on your personal and professional engagement with Indigenous voices and content.

CLASSROOM CONNECTIONS

❷ Leaving Shore

- **Connected Concepts:** Decide on your learning focus. Share the text and its themes with students.

❸ Crossing the Bridge

- **Connecting to Self:** Encourage students to engage in personal reflection.
- **Connecting to Community:** Initiate balanced conversations and deepen understanding through learning circles.
- **Connecting to Land-Based Learning:** Explore activities and experiences that encourage land-based connections.
- **Connecting to Land Back:** Connect contributors' texts to the Land Back movement or reclamation efforts.

❹ Reaching the Shore

- **Connections to Other Indigenous Resources:** Suggest resources to prepare, extend, and enhance learning about Connected Concepts for students in any grade.

❺ Beginning a New Journey

- Encourage students to read the same text through a new lens or read a different text to initiate another journey.

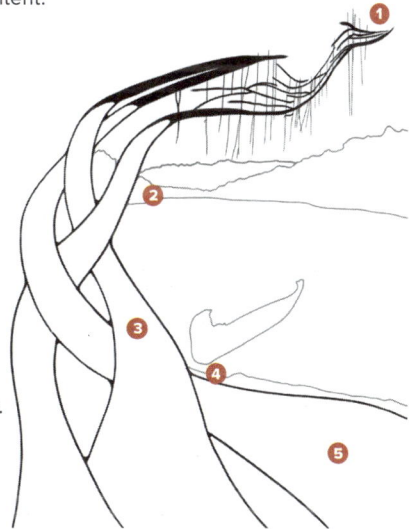

Part Overviews

Each of the book's four parts opens with an overview that prepares you for the journey across the footbridge that connects Indigenous worldviews and the classroom. We continue to think about the importance of readying ourselves for reading and draw upon Jo-ann Archibald Q'um Q'um Xiiem's (Stó:lo and St'át'imc) idea of preparing one's mind, body, and spirit before diving into each section.[1] The part overviews introduce key topics and provide insights into how the contributors embody Indigenous knowing, being, doing, and becoming. We highlight the key connected ideas that surface across the texts featured in each part, noting how the contributors have learned *on* the land, *about* the land, and *from* the land. We introduce the people from whom you will learn and where they are from. While they may come from different places, have individual viewpoints, and use diverse methods of sharing their knowledge, we note the strong ties that connect their work and common actions they have taken. Here, we begin to show the many forms that land-based learning and practice can take, and explore the emotional and spiritual engagements that might encourage readers to become more connected to land. We offer the overviews as a reminder to listen, read, and view with care, considering how you can become ready to learn on and from the land using the texts that follow.

Contributor Biographies

Each contributor's biography is placed before their text to situate the reader in relationship to them. These help us understand where the contributor is coming from and provide insight into where their connections to land are based. We encourage you to include these biographies when sharing the contributors' texts with your class to emphasize that their work and perspectives are integrally connected to place, local knowledge, personal experiences (such as birth and relocation), and where their ancestors are

---

1 Jo-ann Archibald Q'um Q'um Xiiem, "On Becoming Story-Ready," Indigenous Storywork, no date, indigenousstorywork.com/1-for-educators/.

from. Indigenous nations are diverse in their history, language, traditions, and customs, and so are the experiences of Indigenous community members. Read each biography with your class and locate the contributor's ancestral place on a map. They are inviting you into their life and story.

Contributor Narratives and Expressions

Renewal includes essays, photographs, poems, and artworks. Each contributor has used the medium of their choice to communicate their knowledges, perspectives, and experiences related to land and water. The many forms of expression used here have the potential to evoke emotions and provoke new possibilities for you to reimagine your professional practices. The table on pages 34–36 lists each contributor, their nation, and their text.

To engage with visual texts with your whole class, we highly encourage you to use a document camera or project them for all to see. Encourage students to record and share their questions as they view these pieces.

Educator Connections

The Educator Connections section presents our thoughts on each text and encourages you to engage in reflection before sharing the text and its topics with your students.[2] As the topics addressed are sometimes challenging, we encourage you to work through this section to ensure you feel comfortable before approaching these topics with students. The inquiry questions provided here can be used for self-reflection or in discussions with your colleagues in a professional learning community.

---

2   Although we use the terms *educator* and *teacher* here and throughout the book, the Educator Connections section provides opportunities and entry points for any adult learner.

PERSONAL CONNECTIONS

After each text, we explore our own personal connections to it in a conversational narrative that describes how the text relates to our lives, our understandings, and our teaching practice. This is an important first step in learning about Indigenous topics, as it requires us to position ourselves in relation to our learning. We ask ourselves the following big questions: How does this relate to me? Who am I in relation to this topic? We hope our responses serve as examples or starting points, and we encourage you to ask yourself these important questions too. Think of our sharing as the beginning of a conversation. We want to provide our reactions in order to become part of the conversation alongside you. They represent both Indigenous and non-Indigenous perspectives beside one another, which supports the bridging needed for deeper understanding. Our own reflections are an invitation to you to share a raw response—how do you feel immediately after engaging with the text? Consider sharing your responses with your students or colleagues.

EDUCATOR INQUIRY AND ACTIONS

Here, we invite you to engage with each text on a personal and professional level. The texts included in the book are quite short, but are loaded with meaning that can encourage rich, in-depth conversations. We provide guiding questions for inspiration and make suggestions for collaborative inquiry with colleagues—for example, as an action for a professional learning community.

As Rita Bouvier states, "calling oneself *teacher* assumes a relationship with the learner(s) and thus carries immense responsibility for not only the content or knowledge passed on, but also *in practice*."[3] This section guides you in taking on this responsibility, beginning with reflecting on your own educational experiences and ongoing learning and then encouraging you to think and take action. It encourages you to ask the following questions of yourself: How am I bringing Indigenous perspectives and voices into my curriculum? What learning do I need to do to support my work with

---

3   Rita Bouvier, "Poetry as a Cultural Expression," in *Resurgence*, ed. Christine M'Lot and Katya Adamov Ferguson (Portage & Main Press, 2022), 44.

students? Your answers to these questions can be used to guide your actions as you introduce Indigenous voices in your classroom. In schools where we have taught, these questions have also been used to guide action plans for professional learning communities.

Classroom Connections

The Classroom Connections section provides guidance on how to bring the texts to life through questions, prompts, experiences, and resource suggestions. This section follows the trajectory of a unit plan, offering support as you encourage your students to move from initially engaging with the text toward a deeper understanding of the topic.

As an educator, you will interpret these texts in unique ways based on who you are, where you come from, what you think and believe, and how you are situated within the power dynamics and problems being exposed. It is important to anticipate that your students will also have diverse reactions to the texts and interpret them in different ways. We encourage you to openly discuss with students what it feels, sounds, and looks like to respect a story, and how to create a safe space in your classroom for responding to and sharing personal stories. This will help students feel comfortable when participating in the Connecting to Community approach offered in each Classroom Connections section.

Before engaging with each text, it is also essential to identify for students the contributor's nation or homeland, rather than using the general term *Indigenous*. This specificity will allow you to ensure that your content and approach are respectful and accurate.

BEGINNING, BRIDGING, AND BEYOND

We understand that your students will engage with the topics explored in this book at varying levels, depending on their comfort level and prior knowledge and experiences. For this reason, we have indicated whether the prompts and questions provided in the Classroom Connections are at a *Beginning, Bridging*, or *Beyond* phase. We have opted not to align this content with specific grade levels, which do not necessarily indicate experience with or knowledge of Indigenous topics. The Beginning, Bridging, and Beyond phases are described as follows:

> The **Beginning** phase encourages students who are starting out on their journey and have limited experience with or prior knowledge of the topic. This phase is indicated by a crescent-moon icon.

> The **Bridging** phase is for students with some experience with or prior knowledge of the topic. This phase is indicated by a half-moon icon.

● The **Beyond** phase is for students who have extensive experience with or prior knowledge of the topic and are ready for more critical and challenging discussions. This phase is indicated by a full-moon icon.

The phases of the moon support the topic of land-based education, connecting to Mother Earth and the cyclical relationship between land, water, and sky.

CONNECTED CONCEPTS

This section lists three or four underlying topics that are present in the text. Each text provides many possible interconnections and directions for inquiry, but we have chosen to focus on specific big ideas, or Connected Concepts, for each text. For example, while the broad theme of sustainability is addressed in more than one text, we have highlighted multiple ways of taking up that topic. As you step onto the footbridge with students while they begin their learning journey, share the text and topics you want to focus on with them.

Some of the texts deal with subjects and use language that may not be appropriate for younger students. For these learners, you can focus on exploring the Connected Concepts rather than engaging directly with the text. The broader themes and Connected Concepts are accessible and important to students of all ages. See the table on pages 34–36 for the suggested learner level (which takes into consideration both content and reading level) and Connected Concepts for each text. Be sure to review each text before you introduce it to your students.

The Connected Concepts can also be addressed as stand-alone topics to complement other resources you are using. Seek out existing provincial or territorial curricula to supplement and expand on specific topics. This will ensure that Indigenous voices and expressions are central, rather than an add-on. This approach can create more meaningful engagement with Indigenous perspectives and knowledges.

CONNECTING TO SELF: PROMPTS FOR PERSONAL REFLECTION

In this section, we offer questions that encourage students to reflect on the text on both personal and academic levels. Here, students begin taking steps across the footbridge toward greater understanding of Indigenous perspectives. For this work to be relevant, it is important that students consider their own identities. How students demonstrate their learning in this area is up to you; you may invite them to answer questions via written reflection, video reflection, or another mode of assessment. Depending on the topic, you might ask students to discuss these questions with a partner—a less intimidating option than presenting their views in a whole-class discussion. Note that the questions in the Connecting to Self section are provided at the Beginning, Bridging, and Beyond phases.

One way to encourage self-reflection is to pick a prompt for students to consider when beginning to explore the topic, then to come back to it after some further learning to see if, and how, their thinking has changed over time. Using the frame of *learning* and *unlearning* can aid students in seeing these changes.[4] Mi'kmaw scholar Marie Battiste calls for us to make a commitment to *unlearning*, which involves gaining awareness of what has unconsciously become the norm in order to "learn new ways of knowing, valuing others, accepting diversity, and making equity and inclusion foundations for all learners."[5]

CONNECTING TO COMMUNITY: PROMPTS FOR LEARNING CIRCLES

Once students have engaged in a process of personal reflection and introspection, the next step on the footbridge is to engage in conversation with community. This opens our eyes to the various ways in which people experience text. By connecting to community, students will learn about the diverse opinions, experiences, and worldviews of those around them.

One way to facilitate these conversations is through a learning circle, also called a talking circle or sharing circle. Talking circles are traditional processes used by many First Nations to ensure everyone has a voice in decision making, whereas learning circles are a reflective classroom activity that encourages respectful communication, active listening, and unity.

While sitting in a circle, everyone (including the adults in the classroom) is equal. In a learning circle, a specific topic of discussion is chosen, and speakers are encouraged to speak from the heart on this topic. Only the person holding a designated item, such as a talking stick, may speak, while everyone else listens. Speakers talk until they are finished, being respectful of time. Once the speaker has finished, they pass the stick to the person beside them and that person speaks. Not speaking in a learning circle is acceptable; the person simply says "pass" and passes the item on to the next person. The process is complete when everyone has had a chance to speak.

---

4   Marie Battiste, "Nourishing the Learning Spirit: Living Our Way to New Thinking," *Education Canada* 50, no. 1 (2010): 14–18, www.edcan.ca/wp-content/uploads/EdCan-2010-v50-n1-Battiste.pdf.

5   Marie Battiste, *Decolonizing Education: Nourishing the Learning Spirit* (Purich Publishing, 2013), 166.

If you want to use learning circles or a similar process with your students, we encourage you to invite a local Elder or Knowledge Keeper into your classroom to share related nation-specific teachings before doing so. Before trying a learning circle in your classroom, you may want to work through the process with colleagues to increase your comfort level and familiarity.

In the Connecting to Community section, we have provided prompts at the Beginning, Bridging, and Beyond phases that can be used in a learning circle. Choose the prompts that are appropriate for your place of learning. If you are still getting to know your students, start with the Beginning phase prompts; although these may seem simple, you might be surprised at what surfaces in response! You can keep coming back to these prompts and make them part of your routine inside or outside of the classroom.

CONNECTING ONLINE

Post reflections from your own learning or share how you take up these ideas in your educational setting using the hashtags #FootbridgeRenewalBook and #FootbridgeRenewal.

CONNECTING TO LAND-BASED LEARNING

The next step in the learning process is Connecting to Land-Based Learning. This section provides guidance on how to extend learning beyond the classroom, as connecting to land needs to be done in physical, material, and active ways. The suggestions featured here provide possibilities for centring learning *from* the land, *on* the land. The environment where learning takes place is not a neutral background, and classrooms have a certain educational charge. Moving outside with the intention of meaningfully integrating connections to land in student learning is a form of activism that challenges the norms of traditional schooling.

CONNECTING TO LAND BACK

In this section, we delve into the concept of Land Back, a profound and active notion encompassing the return of ancestral lands, reparations, and vital reconnection to the land. Our discussion ties directly to the Land Back movement, offering insights into how each text aligns with critical themes surrounding land dispossession and the enduring impacts of settler colonialism.[6] By surfacing these connections, we ground our conversation in pressing issues related to land. We emphasize the active efforts of Indigenous communities in defending their lands and revitalizing their rights and responsibilities in relation to the land, echoing the words of Tuck and Yang, who remind us that "decolonization is not a metaphor."[7] This section serves as a reminder of the ongoing need for decolonial thinking and actions in the course of our educational journey. Rather than viewing it merely as the transfer of ownership from one property owner to another, we see Land Back as an opportunity to question Western notions of property and how they separated people from their ancestral territories and simultaneously from traditional knowledge systems and relationships. Land Back also prompts us to consider the long-lasting, and in some cases irreversible, damage that has been done to the land and the urgent need to restore relationships to the land. The idea of Land Back is a way of *talking back* to colonialism and *taking back* both land and power. It highlights both historical mistakes and contemporary activism.

Land Back is both straightforward, in terms of the physical restoration of land, and complex, as part of unravelling complicated systems of colonialism and restoring spiritual connections to Mother Earth. These are ideas we are still learning about, and each contributor to this book supports this learning and unlearning. In this section, we identify key disconnections or tensions created by settler colonialism. We focus on treaties, land claims, Land Back resistance efforts, and the historical relationships specific to contributors' ancestral homelands.

---

6   See page 11 for more information on the Land Back movement.

7   Eve Tuck and K. Wayne Yang, "Decolonization Is Not a Metaphor," *Decolonization: Indigeneity, Education & Society* 1, no. 1 (2012): 40.

For settler educators, this section supports becoming more knowledgeable and thinking critically about the reparations needed or already taken in relation to specific territories. It also gives an opportunity to connect to the Land Back movement by providing context related to where the contributor comes from or exploring the disconnections from land that surface through their work. Some contributions connect directly to examples of decolonial activism or identify ways for students and teachers to repair relationships.

CONNECTIONS TO OTHER INDIGENOUS RESOURCES

Finally, at the end of each chapter, we have included a list of resources (that may include books, films, articles, podcasts, and online materials) for further investigation and study. As students take their final steps across the footbridge and reach the shore, they may wish to extend their learning by engaging with these suggested works. The texts we have included may address similar topics, or may have been created by the contributor or an author or artist from the same nation as the contributor. The suggested resources have been created by Indigenous writers, artists, directors, scholars, and thinkers.

If you think a specific text in this book is too challenging for your students, but you would like to teach one of the Connected Concepts, start with one of the age-appropriate resources provided in the Connections to Other Indigenous Resources section. The age and grade ranges provided for each children's and young adult book are based on the publisher's recommendations.

Overview of Narratives and Cultural Expressions

The following table provides an overview of each text, specifying the contributor's name and nation, and the title and type of text. Suggested Learner Level refers to the content and reading level of the text itself; as noted, the Connected Concepts identified for each text can be addressed with students of all ages with various levels of knowledge and experience.

CONTRIBUTOR	CONTRIBUTOR NATION	TITLE OF TEXT	TYPE OF TEXT	SUGGESTED LEARNER LEVEL	CONNECTED CONCEPTS
PART ONE: KNOWING					
Dr. Brian Rice	Kanien'kehá:ka (Mohawk)	*Land-Based Education: A Means to Healthy Learning and Living*	Essay	Grades 9–12 and beyond	• Active lifestyle • Identity • Self-esteem
Nicki Ferland	Red River Métis	*Reclaiming Relationships With Land in the City*	Essay	Grades 9–12 and beyond	• Rural-urban binary • Place names • Belonging and property/ownership
Peatr Thomas	Ininew/ Anishinaabe	*Miskwaadesi Maada Ookii Gikendamowin/ Turtle Sharing Knowledge (From the Sturgeon)*	Artwork and personal essay	Grades 5–12 and beyond	• Pictographs • Oral and visual transmission of culture • Land and water dwellers
Tyna Legault Taylor	Omushkego Cree	*Homelands and Waterways*	Essay	Grades 9–12 and beyond	• Water justice/water and food sovereignty • Environmental racism • Survivance
PART TWO: BEING					
Shannon Webb-Campbell	Mi'kmaq	*"Ecology of Being"*	Poem	Grades 9–12 and beyond	• Selfhood • Interconnectedness • Medicine
Dr. Tasha Beeds	nêhiyaw, Scottish-Métis, and Bajan	*"We Are the Bundle": Activating Indigenous Ancestral Powers*	Essay	Grades 9–12 and beyond	• Ancestry • Kinship • Spiritual bundles

CONTRIBUTOR	CONTRIBUTOR NATION	TITLE OF TEXT	TYPE OF TEXT	SUGGESTED LEARNER LEVEL	CONNECTED CONCEPTS
Sonny Assu	Ligwiłda'xw of the Kwakwaka'wakw Nations	Land Back and Dance as Though the Ancestors Are Watching	Artwork and artist's statement	Grades K–12 and beyond	• Consumerism • Advertising • Critical literacy • Indigenous aesthetics
Class from Jonah Amitnaaq Secondary School (Baker Lake, NU)	Inuit	Qamani'tuaq (ᖃᒪᓂᑦᑐᐊᖅ) Perspectives	Photo essay	Grades K–12 and beyond	• Inuit Qaujimajatuqangit (IQ) • Hunting and fishing sustainably • Perspective • Digital photography
PART THREE: DOING					
shalan joudry	L'nu (Mi'kmaq)	"Raising Forests"	Poem	Grades 5–12 and beyond	• Intergenerational trauma • Environmental protection/stewardship • Environmental degradation
Tricia Logan	Métis	Michif Language Revitalization: Our Lessons On-line and On-land	Essay	Grades 7–12 and beyond	• Language revitalization • Connecting online • Homeland
Dakota Bear	Cree	"Freedom"	Lyrics	Grades 5–12 and beyond	• Idle No More • Sovereignty • Activism • Self-determination
Shirli Ewanchuk	Ojibway	Manitou Akiing/ Spirit Is in the Land	Essay	Grades 9–12 and beyond	• Clothing and textiles • Food and nutrition • Family studies • Geography

CONTRIBUTOR	CONTRIBUTOR NATION	TITLE OF TEXT	TYPE OF TEXT	SUGGESTED LEARNER LEVEL	CONNECTED CONCEPTS
PART FOUR: BECOMING					
Dan Henhawk	Kanien'kehá:ka	*Start First With a Good Mind*	Essay	Grades 9–12 and beyond	• Reimagining leisure • Indigenous ways of doing/being • Learning/unlearning • Sustainability
Réal Carrière	Nehinuw (Swampy Cree) and Métis	*Mah! (Listen!)*	Essay	Grades 9–12 and beyond	• Identity • Ancestral homelands • Worldview
Hetxw'ms Gyetxw (Brett D. Huson)	Gitxsan	*The Art of Learning and Storytelling: "A Gitxsan Ode to Water"*	Artwork and poem	Grades 5–12 and beyond	• Sacredness • Storytelling • Matrilineal society • Water as lifeblood
Reanna McKay (Merasty)	Nîhithaw	*Land Connection for Resurgence and Renewal*	Artwork and artist's statement	Grades K–12 and beyond	• Resurgence • Renewal • Intertwining knowledges • Journeying

PART ONE

KNOWING

THE FIRST SECTION in *Renewal* focuses on *knowing*, providing us with the opportunity to reconsider and renew the ways we think about land. The contributors featured in this section encourage us to think about our own relationships and reactions to the term *land*. By listening deeply to the contributors' individual experiences and perspectives, "to the voices and living stories" (Legault Taylor, page 76), we gain a starting point for our own land-based learning. From here, we can move beyond what we think we know and begin taking small steps, personally and professionally, toward what we would like to learn.

Prepare to learn from the knowledge and perspectives of Dr. Brian Rice (Kanien'kehá:ka), Nicki Ferland (Red River Métis), Peatr Thomas (Ininew/Anishinaabe), and Tyna Legault Taylor (Omushkego Cree). Their individual perspectives on land reflect the resurgence of a broader land-based education, while also encompassing knowledge passed down through previous generations. They share their experiences of growing up and how they came to know what they know through practices such as hunting, fishing, berry picking, cooking and preserving, walking, observing, and listening. They also address tensions in their movement to and from their ancestral territories and how that has shifted their identities and connections to land over time.

Interconnections and wholistic elements are an important aspect of Indigenous ways of knowing. Indigenous ways of knowing about land support how we come to know ourselves, as humans aren't seen as separate from the land, but interconnected with it. In the opening essay, Dr. Brian Rice shares his complex journey to becoming a land-based educator and how reconnecting with the land and adopting an active lifestyle renewed and strengthened his sense of self. For him, as for many of us, the path to more wholistic land-based practices has not been straightforward. On this journey, we may encounter many obstacles and challenges—both internal and external—that affect all aspects of our physical, mental, emotional, and spiritual selves.

As you engage with the contributions in this section, contemplate your relationship with specific places and think about how you acknowledge and categorize these places. Nicki Ferland's essay shows that understanding where Indigenous land was *and still is* located can give us a whole new perspective on the accessibility and context of land-based education. She encourages us to think about being "raised on stories about our roots" (page 54) and to listen back to those stories as a valuable form of knowing and learning.

Peatr Thomas shows us how knowledge can be transmitted over time through a combination of oral stories and images. His artwork takes us back to the spiritual connections depicted in ancient pictographs and describes the contemporary art inspired by them. He encourages us to pay attention to and learn from our interconnections with our animal relatives dwelling on land, in water, or in the sky, and to value their ways of knowing.

Tyna Legault Taylor reminds us that we must understand and acknowledge the impact our actions have on the land for future generations, as she shares the disastrous effects of mining on reserve communities such as her home nation of Attawapiskat. She also emphasizes the spiritual nature of land education, reminding us that water is not just a physical material but is alive with spiritual connections.

This section also introduces the stark ongoing realities of settler colonialism, which are articulated as an opposing force of resistance. This is particularly important for settler educators to keep in mind. Ferland's and Legault Taylor's essays prompt us to reflect on "colonial fiction" and to examine what we believe to be true. Ferland (page 56) describes the myth of the urban/rural binary: "Settlers belong in cities. Indigenous people belong in the wild." Legault Taylor discusses the "fourth-world socio-economic conditions" on her reserve, reminding us that although Canada is a highly developed country, many Indigenous communities have been forced to live in deplorable conditions without clean water.

The contributors' knowledge, ideas, and perspectives create a bridge for us all to walk on by reminding us that land-based learning is accessible.

They prompt us to expand our thinking about the *how* and *where* of land-based learning and encourage us to take up land and water as important issues without limiting ourselves because of funding or location. As you read this section, you may be encouraged to shift your perspective and consider how you can teach from "the other side of the window" (Rice, page 46). Wherever you are, ask yourself, "Do you live and go to school on Indigenous land?" (Ferland, page 56). The answer to this question will ground your journey into land-based education, as you initiate the first few steps.

CONNECTING ONLINE

Post reflections from your own learning or share how you take up these ideas in your educational setting using the hashtags #FootbridgeRenewalBook and #FootbridgeRenewal.

Land-Based Education
A Means to Healthy Learning and Living

DR. BRIAN RICE, an enrolled member of the Mohawk Nation at Kahnawá:ke, Quebec, is a full professor in the Department of Kinesiology and Recreation Management at the University of Manitoba. Over the past 30 years, Brian has been a teacher, an interim principal in an Indigenous-operated school, and an educator in various university faculties. He is the author of three books, including *The Rotinonshonni: A Traditional Iroquoian History Through the Eyes of Teharonhia:wako and Sawiskera,* a Choice Pick of the American Library Association.

———

I AM AN Indigenous land-based educator. I became one when, in 1997 at the age of 41, I walked over 1100 kilometres alone through the Traditional Territory of my people, the Kanien'kehá:ka (Mohawk), as a pretext to writing my doctoral dissertation.[1] I had to be in good health to do so; however, it wasn't always that way.

Growing up, I struggled in school. I never had doubts about my intelligence, but I just couldn't concentrate on the things I was being taught. I would stare out the classroom window for hours and not hear a thing being said. I felt empty inside. I remember wanting to escape from it all. At the same time, I was popular in school and that helped me get through.

In those days, if you did something wrong in school, you were strapped with a belt. My first time being strapped was in grade 1, and in high school I remember the vice-principal strapping me. It hurt, but I tried not to show it. For me, school was like a prison where you got points for good behaviour

---

[1] Brian Rice, *The Rotinonshonni: A Traditional Iroquoian History Through the Eyes of Teharonhia:wako and Sawiskera* (Syracuse University Press, 2016).

and got strapped for bad behaviour. I wanted more than anything to be outside doing things.

My indigeneity wasn't noticeable, but I was always proud of it. When I was young, my parents moved from Buffalo, New York, to a predominantly francophone area of Montreal, and most of my cousins lived in Kahnawá:ke, a Mohawk reserve across the St. Lawrence River. We often visited until my father left us. That differentiated me from a lot of my friends, who had two parents and lived in a house. We lived in a small upstairs apartment, and my mom had to find work to keep us together. I can't say I didn't enjoy my youth, but I felt unfulfilled with my situation and couldn't see a direction out of it.

Around the age of 14, I began to go to taverns, which wasn't unusual for the youth in my area, even though the legal drinking age was 21. When I was 15, I got into a fight in a bar with a guy called "The Hammer." No one got hurt, but when it was over, some of his friends, who were about five years older than me, asked me over for a beer. It was the beginning of a slow slide that led to years of alcoholism. Some of my new friends were criminals. I learned that the criminal mind had no limits toward self-indulgence. It was always all about oneself, and never about anyone else.

My behaviour changed for the worse when I began visiting my father in Buffalo. I was 17, and it had been seven years since he'd left my family. He had been a hero in World War II, then a high steel worker, and he ended up an alcoholic on the streets; however, he was now remarried and in recovery. I wanted to be the way he had been, not the way he was becoming. Around that time, I had my first experience at a university when I attended a beer bash at Concordia University in Montreal and got into a fight with a student. It was like my father's warrior spirit had entered me. I didn't know then that the next eight years would be miserable, as my personal life entered a downward spiral. I couldn't see that most people didn't live like me. Finally, at the age of 26, I decided to get help with my alcohol problem. My eyes were about to be opened to a world of new possibilities.

Free from the distractions that resulted from addiction, I went back to school and slowly began to have some success. In contrast to the subjects and supervision I'd encountered in high school, I preferred the freedom university offered me to study things I liked. I achieved bachelor's and master's degrees in the philosophy of religion. After my previous lifestyle, every

Sunrise at the University of Manitoba.
(Image courtesy of Dr. Brian Rice.)

success seemed worthwhile. I ended up becoming the first Native studies/ social studies teacher in a small Anishnabé school in northern Quebec.

I returned to school by entering a PhD program at McGill University, but, disappointed by a lack of Indigenous content, I transferred to the newly created Traditional Knowledge Program at the California Institute of Integral Studies. Along with academics, Indigenous Elders were our teachers. We completed residencies in California's beautiful redwood forests, as well as in Mexico with Mayan and Nahuatl traditional people and Elders. They took us onto their lands and offered us their perspectives. We always entered their lands in a traditional ceremonial manner, meaning we were "blessed in" by the Elders. We had first-hand experiences in Indigenous ceremonial and historical settings. This was my introduction to land-based learning. I went to Thailand and to Hawaii, where I sailed in a traditional double-hulled canoe with Indigenous Hawaiians. In Senegal, I defended my dissertation at a conference of African healers. To this day, I continue to visit Indigenous Peoples in other parts of the world—Kenya, Myanmar,

Australia, Dominica, Guyana, Japan, and Ireland—to develop relationships with them so that we can connect our common worldviews of our relationships with the lands we come from. We are living in precarious times due to climate change resulting from human activity. Indigenous Peoples' understandings of and care for the environment of their traditional territories are more important for the sustainability of our world than ever.

My own dissertation was the result of my 1100-kilometre walk, which followed the journey of the Peacemaker, who confederated the Kanien'kehá:ka with four other warring nations before bringing them into a peaceful relationship.[2] Completing a traditional knowledge land-based dissertation required me to take different approaches to research. It meant having knowledge of oral traditions and spending time on the land in the places they derived from. This combination of oral traditions and experiential land-based learning allowed me to gain an understanding of place that wouldn't have been possible without walking the land. The walk was my way to earn the right to write my dissertation, which contained both a societal story and a personal one.[3] I think of my walk as a time when I developed a certain emotional maturity. Some might refer to it as a rite of passage.

Today, I teach Indigenous land-based courses at the University of Manitoba. I chose to teach there because they were hiring Indigenous land-based educators, and due to my walk, I believed it was a good fit to pursue similar land-based work in Winnipeg. In my courses in the spring, summer, and fall, I take students on long historical walks and camping and canoeing in and around the city. During the winter, we snowshoe at FortWhyte Alive to the Bison Viewing Mound and build snow shelters. I want my students to not only learn in a healthy manner, but to have meaningful, authentic outdoor experiences in Indigenous settings with nature, history, and culture at the forefront.[4]

---

2   Brian Rice, "Chapter 3: The Kayeneren:kowa (Great Way of Peace)," in *The Rotinonshonni*.

3   Brian Rice, "A Personal Odyssey of Reconciliation: Walking in the Footsteps of the Peacemaker: A Kenienké:haka Land Based Methodology," www.academia.edu/41459848/A_Personal _Odyssey_of_Reconciliation.

4   Editor's note: Several decades ago, Dr. Rice wrote a land-based learning resource, *Indigenous Science: Aki Kwaamdandaa: Aboriginal Environmental Protection Program*, that provided invaluable information about Indigenous science, including psychology, agriculture, astronomy, and forestry.

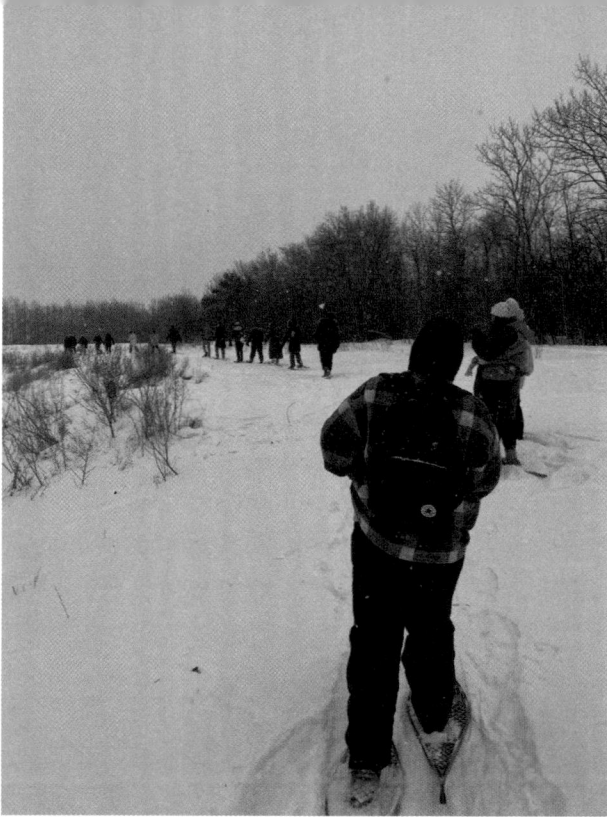

Snowshoeing with students at FortWhyte Alive. (Image courtesy of Dr. Brian Rice.)

My advice for teachers who want to incorporate Indigenous content into their teaching is to be innovative and use the best learning methods you know. Don't be discouraged. There is no better way to demonstrate one's commitment to Indigenous learning than by learning about the Indigenous Peoples whose traditional lands you live on. Seek out knowledge from contemporary Indigenous Knowledge Keepers, understand how to distinguish good from bad historical sources, and search out Indigenous knowledge from archives and other sources.

There are two facets of Indigenous land-based learning that students and teachers should know about when incorporating Indigenous content: there are the stories about the Indigenous people who once lived on the lands we live on today, and the stories of the people who still live on these lands. In my courses, I try to include several facets of land-based knowledge: history, culture, nature, health, and some language. When I need someone to tell the Indigenous story of today, I rely on local Indigenous people. When I need to teach about stories from the past that aren't well known, it sometimes requires more in-depth research from a variety of sources.

My last message is to students struggling in school. My successes only came about when I put away unhealthy things like alcohol, drugs, and cigarettes. They not only kill your spirit, mind, emotions, and body, but they also take away all the potential you have to succeed. Land-based education allows me to teach in a healthy environment outdoors. I am not against the classroom, but some of us, and maybe all of us, need to be stimulated in different ways to have a full learning experience. After 36 years of teaching, I no longer need to stare out the window like I did when I was younger. I am now able to teach on the other side of the window in a healthy outdoor setting. As a person who is now in their late sixties, Indigenous land-based teaching and learning helps keep me healthy and active—and it will do the same for anyone who wishes to take part in it.

Educator Connections

Read the editors' thoughts and engage in reflection. Respond to the questions that follow on your own or with your colleague(s).

PERSONAL CONNECTIONS

Christine: Dr. Brian Rice is someone I personally and professionally look up to, as he was my first Indigenous teacher (who I didn't encounter until I attended the University of Winnipeg, where he taught an Indigenous education course). I enjoyed reading his narrative essay to learn more about his background and school experiences. When he reminisced about how he would "stare out of the classroom window for hours and not hear a thing being said," I chuckled because I know many students who do this. I hope this book provides both Indigenous and non-Indigenous educators with inspiration for land-based educational activities that not only get students outside of the four walls of the classroom, but also promote healthy living and lifestyles. When I read Brian's reflections on his past negative lifestyle, I felt my resolve deepen that as educators, our job is not just to teach students the subjects, but also how to live a good life. It was through such a lens that this book was shaped.

Katya: Dr. Brian Rice's challenges were transformed into great accomplishments through reconnecting with land. His story and struggles nudge me toward deeper understanding of my own father's challenges. My dad also had challenges with traditional academic settings; he would have been caught staring out the classroom window. He used to tell a story of ripping up one of his report cards and putting it down the sewer because he was too embarrassed to bring it home. But if his teachers had asked him what he was staring at, they would likely have heard observations and hypothesizing about animals and the natural world. In later years, his alcoholism took hold of his potential, his body and mind, and almost his spirit. He found the greatest balance when connecting to natural environments—most often in the boreal forest or on the water. A year after my dad passed away, I had the privilege to walk alongside Brian during a land-based course at the University of Manitoba. For me, the walks were filtered through a lens of grief. They helped me process ideas from my dad about the interconnections between living beings and the importance of balance in one's life. Walking helped me see connections between the places where we walked and the histories of those lands and waters. I felt unexpected connections to the past and present.

EDUCATOR INQUIRY AND ACTIONS

- What is your connection to the land you are on? Has the length of time you or your ancestors have been here influenced this connection? If so, how?

- Describe shifts you can make in your teaching practice so that some of your teaching happens on the "other side of the window." Plan small changes to your routines.

- Dr. Brian Rice shares, "There is no better way to demonstrate one's commitment to Indigenous learning than by learning about the Indigenous Peoples whose traditional lands you live on." Share your thoughts about this statement. What are you committed to learning more about (or who do you want to learn from) in your professional learning community?

- This essay brings up important tensions and questions such as: Can land-based knowledges and Indigenous knowledges transfer to places beyond where they originated? How? Are there certain practices that support land-based learning across different places? How does your ancestry affect your perspective and learning experiences?

- Take a walk with your class or colleagues. How does walking support a "renewal" of your perspective, goals, feelings, or actions in relation to the land?

- As a school team, take time to research the traditional territories you are on. Where does the current name come from? What is the traditional name? What agreements led to settlement on this land, if any? Practise correctly pronouncing the name in an Indigenous language.

- How does Dr. Brian Rice's story connect to your personal life? What did you learn from him about being a land-based educator?

- Dr. Brian Rice advises teachers who want to incorporate Indigenous content "to be innovative and use the best learning methods you know. Don't be discouraged." Write some of your main considerations or worries regarding teaching Indigenous content as an Indigenous or non-Indigenous educator. Brainstorm some innovative things you are already doing in your teaching and how you can use these to address your concerns.

Classroom Connections

Introduce to students the narrative and the Connected Concepts you wish to focus on. Use the following questions, prompts, and resource suggestions to guide student learning.

CONNECTED CONCEPTS

- Active lifestyle
- Identity
- Self-esteem

CONNECTING TO SELF: PROMPTS FOR PERSONAL REFLECTION

) **Beginning**

- How does being on the land/being outside make you feel?

- What are some aspects of school that you enjoy? What are some aspects you dislike?

) **Bridging**

- What are some healthy habits you practise every day or want to begin practising?

- Are there things that distract you from your schoolwork or hobbies? What are they?

● **Beyond**

- Reflect on healthy choices you have made in your life. How would you describe the path you took to making these choices?

- How has your education addressed Indigenous content so far? Do you think it has been adequate? Why or why not?

CONNECTING TO COMMUNITY: PROMPTS FOR LEARNING CIRCLES

) **Beginning**

- Share one thing you love about being outside. It could be a specific place, or something you like to see or do (such as a game).

- Share a way you can show kindness or respect to your classmates. It could be something you've done or would like to do, or something someone else has done for you.

) **Bridging**

- After taking a walk as a class, come together to share what you learned along the way.

- Think back to a time when your culture was or was not noticeable and how that made you feel. Describe how you navigated and responded to those feelings.

● **Beyond**

- Drawing on Dr. Brian Rice's descriptions, discuss the ways ceremony can play a role in land-based education.

- Describe some missed learning opportunities you've had throughout your school experiences. Think of some ways a particular teacher could have engaged you more or better supported your self-esteem.

CONNECTING TO LAND-BASED LEARNING

❭ **Beginning**

- Research and locate the traditional territories of Dr. Brian Rice's people, the Kanien'kehá:ka (Mohawk). On the Native Land Digital website <native-land.ca/maps/territories/mohawk/>, check out the map of Kanien'kehá:ka territory, which stretches across the Canada–US border and into New York State.

❱ **Bridging**

- Think back to an experience of travelling to a new place—or, better yet, plan to go to a new place with your classmates. Work as a group to learn about the place together. How can you enter familiar or unfamiliar territory better informed about the promises made there and with greater reverence for the land?

● **Beyond**

- Take a walk to your former elementary, middle, or high school. A physical walk would be ideal, but you could also take a walk back in your mind. Imagine staring outside the window during your own school experiences or, if you were like Dr. Brian Rice and did spend time looking outside, recall what you saw. Alternatively, look outside a window at home or at school. Take a few minutes to jot down as many questions as you can about what you see or imagine. Then step outside and try to answer your questions. When you come back inside, write down any new questions you have.

CONNECTING TO LAND BACK

- The Kanien'kehá:ka (Mohawk) make up the Eastern part of the Haudenosaunee Confederacy. The Haudenosaunee are also known as "People of the Longhouse."[5] It is important to note that legal processes and government existed in Haudenosaunee society and other Indigenous nations prior to colonization. According to the Kahnawà:ke Branch of the Mohawk Nation, "the Haudenosaunee are a constitutional democracy that has existed since time immemorial and long before the colonial occupation of settler states such as Canada and the United States. The Haudenosaunee are governed by an ancient constitution known as the Kaianere'kó:wa; the Great Law of Peace."[6] After explorers came to this territory, treaties were created and represented in the form of wampum belts, which were used to mark agreements between peoples. Wampum are beads made of shells, which were threaded together in complex ways to represent agreements and other significant information.

  Research the history of wampum belts as physical expressions of treaties. Look up the Two Row Wampum Belt (Kaswentha), for example, which symbolizes an agreement between the Haudenosaunee and the European newcomers. What lessons do the wampum teach us about Land Back efforts? How did differing worldviews contribute to misunderstandings about the spirit of the treaties signed between the Haudenosaunee and colonial governments? What tensions still exist there?

CONNECTIONS TO OTHER INDIGENOUS RESOURCES

Books

Just a Walk, by Jordan Wheeler (Theytus Books, 2010; ages 3–5).
This rhyming picture book explores how the world opens up to a young boy as he connects with nature.

---

5   "Kahnawà:ke Branch of the Mohawk Nation," Haudenosaunee: Kahnawake Branch of the Mohawk Nation, Six Nation Iroquois Confederacy, www.kahnawakelonghouse.com/.

6   "Kahnawà:ke Branch of the Mohawk Nation," Haudenosaunee: Kahnawake Branch of the Mohawk Nation.

Walking Together, by Elder Albert D. Marshall and Louise Zimanyi (Annick Press, 2023; ages 4–7).
This picture book celebrates land and water from a Mi'kmaw perspective, exploring respectful and reciprocal relationships between humans, plants, animals, and other-than-human beings.

The Kodiaks: Home Ice Advantage, by David A. Robertson (HighWater Press, 2024; ages 9–12).
This middle-grade novel explores themes of identity, belonging, self-esteem, and physical and mental health through the experiences of Alex, an 11-year-old Cree boy. The accompanying teacher guide helps educators navigate how to address the ongoing impacts of colonialism.

Seeing the World with Aboriginal Eyes: A Four Directional Perspective on Human and Nonhuman Values, Cultures and Relationships on Turtle Island, by Brian Rice (Aboriginal Issues Press, 2005).
This book is geared toward adult readers who want to learn more about Indigenous worldviews including cosmology, environment, and ceremonies.

Online

Kanienhehá:ka Creation Story, adapted from a story by Ionataié:was, Mohawk storyteller (Mohawk Language Custodian Association – Kontinonhstats, 2016). <www.kanehsatakevoices.com/wp-content/uploads /2017/04/CREATION_-as-told-by-KANIENKEHAKA-woman-storyteller -FINAL2-April-13.pdf>.
This presentation tells the story of how Turtle Island came to be.

"Mohawk Council of Kahnawake 'repulsed' by politicization of Habs' land acknowledgment," The Canadian Press, CBC News, October 20, 2021. <www.cbc.ca/amp/1.6218440>.
This article describes a debate over Montreal as unceded territory that ensued after a land acknowledgment made by the Montreal Canadiens before an NHL game.

ôtênaw, produced, directed, and edited by Conor McNally, 2017. <vimeo
.com/203909985>.
This video highlights the oral storytelling and wisdom of Dr. Dwayne Don-
ald (Papaschase Cree), an associate professor at the University of Alberta.
He describes the importance of walking as a life practice and his perspective of kinship relationships.

Territorial Acknowledgement, Concordia University, Indigenous Directions.
<www.concordia.ca/indigenous/resources/territorial-acknowledgement
.html>.
This is a great resource for creating a land acknowledgment and provides
information about the Kanien'kehá:ka Nation and their stewardship and
care for the lands and waters around what is known now as Montreal.

The Wampum Chronicles, by Darren Bonaparte..
This site offers images of wampum belts and historical information, as well
as links to articles and historical documents.

"What Land Back Means for This Reclamation Camp," by Ka'nhehsí:io Deer,
CBC News, July 18, 2021. <newsinteractives.cbc.ca/longform/what-land
-back-means-for-this-reclamation-camp-in-kahnawake/>.
This article shares how a Mohawk community is actively resisting new housing development on their territory.

Reclaiming Relationships
With Land in the City

NICKI FERLAND is a Two-Spirit Red River Métis mother, wife, aunty, and helper. She is an educator, writer, and researcher whose work focuses on Métis women and Two-Spirit people and their relationships with land in Winnipeg. Her parents are both descended from scrip-bearing Métis families with ancestral roots in St. Vital and St. Boniface (Winnipeg) and Lorette, Manitoba. Nicki is the Director of Land-Based Education and Indigenous Curriculum at the University of Manitoba and is currently working toward completing her PhD in Education.

———

I GREW UP in the small Métis village of Lorette, Manitoba, about 30 kilometres southeast of Winnipeg. We tended a huge backyard garden from spring to fall. We hunted deer and fished from freshwater lakes in sun and snow alike. We picked vegetables, fruit, and berries, then made pies, preserves, and pickles. In the summers, we gathered together with extended networks of grandparents, aunties, uncles, and dozens of cousins. We had deep relationships with land and community in Lorette, and I was raised on stories about our roots. My paternal great-great-grandparents, Sarah Goulet and Elzéar Lagimodière, helped establish the community with other Métis farmers and buffalo hunters in the 1850s. We've lived there ever since.

When I was about 10 years old, my mom and I moved to the big city. I was a country girl, uprooted and transplanted at the beginning of my adolescence. Although my 10-year-old self wouldn't or couldn't articulate it, in the city I felt disconnected from land—displaced. I didn't feel rooted to this land, to the seasonal cycles and patterns that drove our way of life in Lorette, to place, to my ancestors, to our *Traditional* Territory. Nothing I learned in school or elsewhere opposed the deeply ingrained implicit narratives that cities are settler spaces, and Indigenous people don't belong in them.

I was well into my twenties, at university, when I started connecting back to my Métis identity, culture, land, and community. That was the start of a journey of coming to know the ancestral and nation-based relationships I held with land and place in the city,[1] learning about the Indigenous origins of cities across North America and seeing urban places and urban Indigenous people through a different lens. It has taken a decade of unlearning to see the city for what it is: Indigenous land—altered, covered up, appropriated, but nonetheless Indigenous land.

As an Indigenous person moving from a rural area, it was difficult for me to connect with land in the city, but even Indigenous people born and raised in cities express a sense of disconnection with urban land.[2] Indigenous people, along with settlers and more recent newcomers, have internalized colonial narratives that suggest Indigenous people don't belong in cities; we belong in rural villages and remote reserve communities. Cities are settler spaces that were built by settlers for settlers, or so the story goes. This narrative is corroborated by the ideas that land is fundamentally different within city limits (i.e., no longer Indigenous), and that city-dwelling Indigenous people are less *authentically* Indigenous than our rural and reserve counterparts and "supposedly disconnected to Indigenous homelands and sacred places."[3]

The colonial fiction (or fantasy, perhaps) that city land is somehow different, that land transforms at the perimeter of the city and ceases to be Indigenous, is supported by another colonial construction: the urban-rural binary. According to the binary—which is used to geographically, socially, and ecologically map land, place, and people—*urban* and *rural* have assigned

---

1   My paternal ancestors who established Lorette had moved there from St. Boniface, a Métis community located in present-day Winnipeg. My maternal ancestors had a Red River lot in St. Vital, another historic Métis community and the neighbourhood where I grew up; my great-great-great-grandfather was MLA for St. Vital in the 1869 provisional government and was elected to that seat in the first Manitoba Legislature, from 1870–74. My ancestors, including the Lagimodières, the Grants, the Goulets, the Poitras, and the Beauchemins, to name a few, figured in several significant moments that shaped the city.

2   Nicki Ferland, "'We're Still Here': Teaching and Learning About Métis Women's and Two-Spirit People's Relationships With Urban Land in Winnipeg" (Master's thesis, University of Saskatchewan, 2022), harvest .usask.ca/handle/10388/13931.

3   Megan Bang et al., "Muskrat Theories, Tobacco in the Streets, and Living Chicago as Indigenous Land," *Environmental Education Research* 20, no. 1 (2014): 37–55, doi.org/10.1080/13504622.2013.865113.

values and clear boundaries. Indigenous people *fit* in one space and are *anomalous* to the other.[4] Settlers belong in cities. Indigenous people belong in the wild. This in turn reinforces an urban-rural-reserve hierarchy of Indigenous land and Indigeneity (defined perhaps by one's connection or access to Indigenous land-based knowledges and practices). The binary, however, ignores the ways in which Indigenous geographies connect the urban and non-urban[5]—Indigenous people have always lived and travelled in and between rural and (increasingly) urban spaces. In fact, when Indigenous people migrate to the city, many are still living within their traditional territories.[6]

Before the pandemic, I had an opportunity to facilitate land-based programming for a mostly Indigenous group of high school students in an urban neighbourhood with a large Indigenous demographic. Their school plays the national anthem over the loudspeakers every morning (sometimes in Indigenous languages), followed by a land acknowledgment. When we first met, I asked the students, "Do you live and go to school on Indigenous land?" All but one out of the 20 answered "no." It was a moment of frustration and purpose, because I understood the repercussions of growing up disconnected, without a relationship with land, and the resulting sense of isolation, detachment, and uncertainty about being Indigenous in the city. It highlighted a need for more land-based education focused on helping learners reclaim relationships and re-story cities as Indigenous land.

The myths about Indigenous land and people in the city are rooted in settler colonial history. Take Winnipeg, for example, which is fairly important in the history of settler colonial expansion across the northwest.[7] First Nations, and later the Métis Nation, settled in the area seasonally and had deep relationships with this land and with the specific place at the junction of the Red and Assiniboine Rivers. History, however, only recognizes

4 Heather Dorries, "'Welcome to Winnipeg': Making Settler Colonial Urban Space in 'Canada's Most Racist City,'" in *Settler City Limits: Indigenous Resurgence and Colonial Violence in the Urban Prairie West*, ed. Heather Dorries et al. (University of Manitoba Press, 2019), 25–43.

5 Julie Tomiak et al., "Settler City Limits," in *Settler City Limits: Indigenous Resurgence and Colonial Violence in the Urban Prairie West*, ed. Heather Dorries et al. (University of Manitoba Press, 2019), 1–21.

6 Tracy L. Friedel, "Looking for Learning in All the Wrong Places: Urban Native Youths' Cultured Response to Western-Oriented Place-Based Learning," *International Journal of Qualitative Studies in Education* 24, no. 5 (2011): 531–46, doi.org/10.1080/09518398.2011.600266.

7 Owen Toews, *Stolen City: Racial Capitalism and the Making of Winnipeg* (ARP Books, 2018).

permanency and property—if you do not pay for it and put a (real or metaphorical) fence around it, it doesn't count. The city's official origin story begins with the colonial fur trade: By 1812, the Selkirk Settlers had arrived and established the Red River colony. They named the capital (which would become part of the future city of Winnipeg) Assiniboia, after the Assiniboine or Nakoda people who resided there.[8] In 1873, Winnipeg—its name derived from the Cree *win nipi*, meaning "dirty water"[9]—was incorporated as the capital of the new province of Manitoba. The name *Manitoba* stemmed from an Anishinaabe term meaning "where Creator sits." These place names speak to the relationships First Nations have with this place.

During this period, Indigenous people living in the Red River settlement greatly outnumbered the settlers (22 to 3, according to the 1870 census). The area was literally shaped by its Indigenous inhabitants. City road maps contain a great deal of evidence pointing to the influence and role that Indigenous people had in urban development. In what would become the city of Winnipeg, land routes mirrored the water routes. Examples include the Métis overland cart trails (part of present-day Pembina Highway and Portage Avenue) as well as Crow Wing Trail, which lies next to the Red River in the historic St. Vital neighbourhood, and another Anishinaabe horse trail that runs along the Assiniboine River, which is present-day Wellington Crescent. Other unique features of Winnipeg's roads (the wide streets and the Pembina-Corydon Interchange, famously known as Confusion Corner, as examples) are remnants of the Red River cart era that continue to influence the ways we navigate the city today. City routes are Indigenous routes that teach us about Indigenous roots.

---

8 Assiniboine is an *exonym* (the name others call them) and Nakoda is an *endonym* (the name they call themselves).

9 In his essay collection *Winipêk: Visions of Canada from an Indigenous Centre* (McClelland & Stewart, 2024, p. 11), Niigaan Sinclair notes that Wînipêk is a Cree and Anishinaabe word derived from *wiinad*, meaning "dirty," and *nibiing*, meaning "waters."

Prairie cities were literally constructed around existing Indigenous communities,[10] but I don't remember learning about the roles of Indigenous people in early urbanization across the prairies, or about the fact that Anishinaabe and Métis people helped build the road (Dawson's Trail) that brought settlers west to nascent Winnipeg—maybe I missed that day? Indigenous people were eventually driven from the city, and from then on, the idea of the settler city and the story of its settler origins became deeply ingrained in urban consciousness. Nowadays, Indigenous place is recognized at, sanctioned in, and restricted to a few specific historic urban sites, reinforcing the idea that Indigenous land is confined to limited small pockets of the city and is not all-encompassing.[11] But this is all Indigenous land, and Indigenous people are still here.

I had internalized the ideas that cities aren't Indigenous and that urban Indigenous people are *less authentically* Indigenous than my rural and reserve peers, and I was inadvertently reinforcing these myths as a land-based educator. Like others, I took students out of the city and into the bush to learn on the land, or looked for places in the city that most resembled nature (parks and urban forests). I work on an urban campus that is located on Métis Red River lots, an overland cart trail, and the beaten path of an old horse trail. But I consistently removed students from that land, from the city. Why? Is it not still Indigenous land? Most cities have been effectively covered with concrete and built structures, designed to obscure Indigenous land and inhibit relationship-building (as if that is only possible in green spaces). But that campus is Indigenous land. Cities are Indigenous land.

When we remove students from the city to learn on the land or imply that only urban forests and city parks remain *land*, we're implicitly reinforcing the colonial narratives about urban Indigenous land and people. Learning on the land can happen in learners' own backyards, on their schoolyards and campuses, and in neighbourhoods across cities. Urban land-based education helps city-dwelling Indigenous learners reclaim relationships with

---

10 Brenda Macdougall, cited in Tyler McCreary, "Urban Métis Communities: The Politics of Recognition, Reflexivity, and Relationality," in *Settler City Limits: Indigenous Resurgence and Colonial Violence in the Urban Prairie West*, ed. Heather Dorries et al. (University of Manitoba Press, 2019), 151–72.

11 Robert Coutts, *Authorized Heritage: Place, Memory, and Historic Sites in Prairie Canada* (University of Manitoba Press, 2021).

urban land and community, re-story cities as Indigenous land, and foster a sense of connection and belonging.

Educator Connections

Read the editors' thoughts and engage in reflection. Respond to the questions that follow on your own or with your colleague(s).

PERSONAL CONNECTIONS

Christine: Nicki Ferland's essay really resonates with me, because as an Indigenous person growing up in the city, I too felt disconnected from the land. Every summer when I was growing up, my mom and aunties would take my sister and me to Swan Lake, where we would go to the reserve to watch the annual powwow and visit with extended family. I remember feeling connected to land and place only then—never in the city. Nicki's explanation of how the hidden curriculum in schools teaches us that "cities are settler spaces that were built by settlers for settlers" articulates my feelings of disconnection. I appreciate this essay for telling a story I also never learned in school, particularly about the roles of Indigenous people in early urbanization. Nicki's essay has ignited in me an excitement for urban land-based education that I didn't know was possible. Sign me up for a walking tour of the city!

Katya: Nicki Ferland's essay helps me understand more about the city of Winnipeg where I grew up. I have been trying to understand Winnipeg's Indigenous roots, and have found lots of value in learning about land in urban locations. As a settler, doing this helps me see the impacts of settler colonialism more clearly. For example, in the summer of 2023 I facilitated a walk and art workshop at The Forks in Winnipeg with students from the University of Manitoba. We used soil to create an art installation representing a turtle that was intended to connect to stories of Turtle Island as well as to truths about place as interpreted by the students who participated. The intention of our urban public art was to teach, to bring attention to the ongoing Indigenous presence in this location, and to encourage reflection about the histories of past, present, and future. However, it was not welcomed. After its completion, we were questioned by the authorities of this historic site and told that what we had done was prohibited. It signalled to me that, although this is a major historic site recognized for Indigenous history and as a place of Indigenous-settler relations, it is still dominated by settler colonial views of land.

EDUCATOR INQUIRY AND ACTIONS

- Consider the location of your school or community. Is it considered urban, rural, or reserve, or something in between?

- Take a walk around your school or workplace with the new perspectives shared by Nicki Ferland in mind. What changes could you make to your school or work environment to explicitly signal that this is an Indigenous place?

- With your colleagues, compile what you know collectively about your city or town's history. How is "the story of its settler origins...deeply ingrained in urban consciousness"?

- How can you encourage city-dwelling students to "reclaim relationships with urban land and community"?

- Think about the ways you and your class or community can help re-story cities as Indigenous land.

- Share with your school team how the idea of urban land-based education expands possibilities in your teaching. Find a colleague who wants to venture into taking their teaching and learning into the urban environment and plan your first three experiences together.

Classroom Connections

Introduce to students the narrative and the Connected Concepts you wish to focus on. Use the following questions, prompts, and resource suggestions to guide student learning.

CONNECTED CONCEPTS

- Rural-urban binary
- Place names
- Belonging and property/ownership

CONNECTING TO SELF: PROMPTS FOR PERSONAL REFLECTION

Beginning

- What are some activities you have done with your family? Who taught or guided you as you did these activities?

- What are some ways you are connected to seasonal cycles and patterns?

Bridging

- Have you ever felt uprooted or transplanted? How did you react to this?

- Why are place names important? Have you observed any changes to place names where you live?

Beyond

- In what urban places do you feel connected to nature and land?

- What are some of the traditional names for the spaces you occupy?

CONNECTING TO COMMUNITY: PROMPTS FOR LEARNING CIRCLES

Beginning

- Share an outdoor place you feel connected to and explain why you feel connected to that place.

- Nicki Ferland describes a deep relationship with land. Share a word to describe your relationship with land and explain why you chose that word.

Bridging

- Share a story of feeling disconnected from or reconnected to land.

- Share your knowledge of the history of the place you live and how it came to be.

Beyond

- Discuss the differences between belonging and ownership.

- Discuss the impact of the "deeply ingrained implicit narratives that cities are settler spaces" taught in schools and elsewhere.

CONNECTING TO LAND-BASED LEARNING

Beginning

- Go outdoors and select a tree or other plant. Think about or observe how this plant is influenced by the elements throughout the seasons.

- Learn the traditional Indigenous names for various animals, plants, and other elements of nature you see outside.

Bridging

- Visit the website Whose Land <www.whose.land> and explore the traditional lands of Indigenous nations. Whose land are you on? What were the original agreements made on this land?

- Go outdoors and pay attention to the natural world around you. Choose one natural item and create a name for it that reflects its characteristics and your relationship to it. For example, you might choose "yellow friendly flower" as your name for a dandelion. Explore an Indigenous name for your item and any traditional uses for it.

Beyond

- Visit Google Maps and look at the area where you live. What sites of Indigenous historical significance (place names, petroglyphs/pictographs, ceremonial sites, cultural centres, or landmarks) are located there? How close are you to significant waterways or natural formations?

- Nicki Ferland shares that in the case of Winnipeg, Manitoba, "City road maps contain a great deal of evidence pointing to the influence and role that Indigenous people had in urban development." Find evidence in the form of archives, maps, public records, stories, interviews, and so on that shows the role Indigenous people played in urban development in a city of interest to you.

CONNECTING TO LAND BACK

- Nicki Ferland encourages us to "see the city for what it is: Indigenous land—altered, covered up, appropriated, but nonetheless Indigenous land." Indigenous people don't need to leave the city to be Indigenous, as urban land is ancestral land. Ferland brings attention to the disconnections created by the urban-rural binary that create a harmful border between Indigenous Peoples and land. In addition, reserves created as a result of settler colonial power and control have caused further divisions.

  Ferland's work supports the Land Back movement by conceptualizing the reclamation of land as something we can do in our everyday thinking by shifting the way we see cities. How can we encourage this sense of belonging and relationship to urban lands both within ourselves and among our friends and family?

CONNECTIONS TO OTHER INDIGENOUS RESOURCES

Books

A Girl Called Echo Omnibus, by katherena vermette (HighWater Press, 2023; ages 12–18).
This combined volume collects the four-part graphic novel series, which focuses on a Métis teenager pulled into time-travel adventures where she experiences pivotal events in Métis history.

Little Moons, by Jen Storm (HighWater Press, 2024; ages 12–18).
This graphic novel explores grief through the lens of Reanna, an Ojibwe teenager mourning the loss of her older sister. When her mother moves to the city, Reanna is confronted with the differences between the urban setting and her life on the reserve.

Surviving the City series, by Tasha Spillett (HighWater Press, 2018–2024; ages 12 and up).
This three-part graphic novel series explores themes of identity, friendship, colonialism, and living in an urban centre as Indigenous people.

Wînipêk: Visions of Canada from an Indigenous Centre, by Niigaan Sinclair (McClelland & Stewart, 2024).
This book of essays focuses on Winnipeg, connecting to themes of belonging, property ownership, and the significance of place names. It works toward understanding shifting perspectives of rural and urban places as Indigenous territories.

Online
"Journey to Naawi-Oodena: Part 1," Treaty One Development Corporation. <treaty1.ca/videos/>.
Providing an example of what Land Back might look like in an urban centre, this video shares historical information and future plans for a new urban development in Winnipeg led by the seven First Nations who are signatories of Treaty 1.

Miskwaadesi Maada Ookii Gikendamowin/ Turtle Sharing Knowledge (From the Sturgeon)

PEATR THOMAS is an Ininew and Anishinaabe self-taught visual artist from the Pimicikamak and Miskwewe Ziibi territories. Peatr shares his knowledge and culture through his art, which blends traditional teachings and stories with contemporary painting skills and practices. Street art helped him find his voice as he adjusted to city life after leaving the reserve, and he hopes to give youth the same inspiration he felt looking at colourful murals many years ago.

———

*Miskwaadesi Maada Ookii Gikendamowin/Turtle Sharing Knowledge
(From the Sturgeon)*
Digital Image
(Image courtesy of Peatr Thomas.)

THE STURGEON are Knowledge Keepers of our ancestors, for they have been around since the age of dinosaurs. The Sturgeon remind us to keep the water clean and healthy, and share with us, the Land Dwellers, the responsibility to keep it this way.

In the Sacred Seven Ancestor Teachings, the Painted Turtle represents Truth.[1] This being is a Land Dweller, but they live most of their lives in fresh water. They understand both worlds.

In the water, the Sturgeon connects with other water beings to find a solution to pollution and to people forgetting their culture. The Sturgeon decides which teachings to share so that the Land Dwellers may put forth an effort to preserve healthy waters. The Sturgeon knows the Turtle will speak and knows nothing but the Truth, so trusts them with this ancient knowledge.

When the Turtle hears the Sturgeon's call, they dive down to listen to the Sturgeon's message and teachings. As the Turtle emerges, they rest on a fallen tree to wait for passing Land Dwellers to hear their message. We have to be observant to see the Painted Turtle and be willing to listen to hear their message and teachings.

LAND AND WATER: WHERE DO "SPIRIT LINES" FIT IN?

A common visual element used in Indigenous art is what are commonly called Spirit Lines. These are often used to show visual connections.

---

1 Edward Benton-Banai, Wisconsin Ojibway of the Fish Clan and spiritual teacher of the Lac Court Ori- elles Band of the Ojibway Tribe, shared these Seven Teachings (Love, Bravery, Humility, Honesty, Respect, Wisdom, Truth) in *The Mishomis Book: The Voice of the Ojibway*, first published by Indian Country Press in 1979. The book is still available from the University of Minnesota Press.

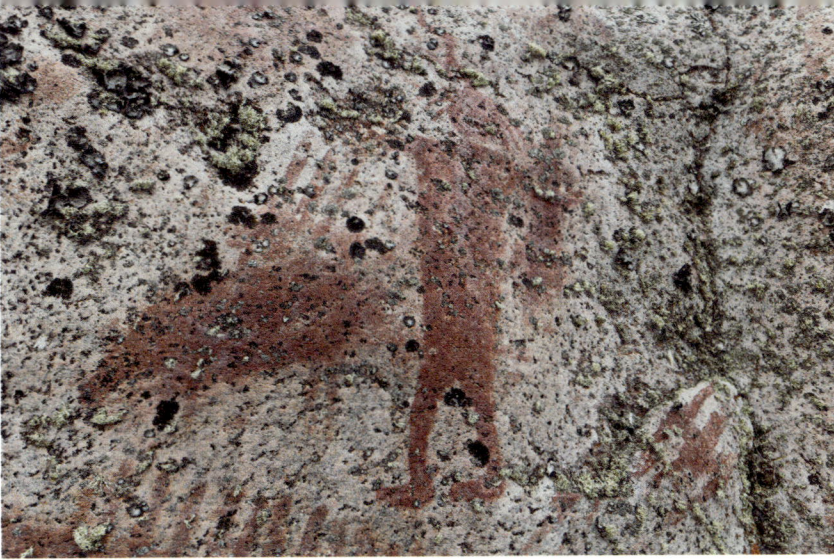

Pictograph at Artery Lake, Bloodvein River waterway, Pimachiowin Aki.
Photo credit: Lorne Coulson (used with permission).

Anishinaabe artist Norval Morrisseau commonly used Spirit Lines in his paintings, and is said to have been one of the first Indigenous artists to include these in modern contemporary art.

Many Indigenous artists have since used Spirit Lines in their work. My understanding is that all artists creating new works today draw inspiration from artworks they admire, and chances are, the artists who created those artworks drew inspiration from someone they admired, and so forth. I believe this cycle has continued for thousands of years. I had never heard any explanation of the origin of Spirit Lines beyond that of artists drawing inspiration from existing art, such as Morrisseau's.

As an Indigenous artist, I did not want to draw inspiration from existing modern works of art unless I truly understood what I was painting. To use Spirit Lines in my work, I had to find a deeper meaning to their purpose and even their origin.

When I was a child in Bloodvein First Nation (my mother's homelands), my uncle took us up the Bloodvein River to look at pictographs, ancient rock paintings. The river system runs from the east side of Lake Winnipeg in Manitoba into Ontario, with its waterways reaching as far as Lake Superior. Along the river is one of the largest collections of pictographs on Turtle Island. They are thousands of years old.[2]

---

2   "The Land That Gives Life: Cultural Sites," Pimachiowin Aki World Heritage Site, pimaki.ca/the-land-that-gives-life/cultural-sites/.

Over the last decade, I have studied images of the Bloodvein River pictographs, mainly to understand the placement and direction of the painted lines. One day, I noticed one particular pictograph depicting a person holding something, with a wavy line emanating from their head—a Spirit Line, one might say. I figured this could be one of the images that inspired later artists to depict Spirit Lines and symbols of connection.

After observing the potential source for Spirit Lines, I wondered why they were represented using wavy lines. I had to think about the simpler life Indigenous Peoples lived thousands of years ago and how they would visualize and represent the things they practised with one simple stroke of paint on a rock.

How did people thousands of years ago easily connect to each other and distant places?

The answer is water. With the forests being so dense, the easiest way to travel was by water, and perhaps this was one way they visualized connection. The curves of Spirit Lines seem to closely resemble the shape of a waterway traversing the landscape. In my research, I have not yet seen anyone else make this connection or express this understanding of Spirit Lines.

With this new understanding, I have started to include Spirit Lines within my artworks. In "Miskwaadesi Maada Ookii Gikendamowin/Turtle Sharing Knowledge (From the Sturgeon)," the light blue lines show the Sturgeon connecting with each other. I visually represent Land and Water, where Spirit Lines are present.

Educator Connections

Read the editors' thoughts and engage in reflection. Respond to the questions that follow on your own or with your colleague(s).

PERSONAL CONNECTIONS

Christine: I've seen Peatr Thomas in action creating street art based on Indigenous knowledges, and I love watching him meticulously work to bring colour and hope to neighbourhoods. I think it's cool how he transmits cultural knowledge through street art—a modern practice modelled from an ancient one. I had never heard of spirit lines before, and I appreciate reading about Peatr's thought process as he tried to understand how our ancient relatives related to other living beings.

Katya: Peatr Thomas's artwork is stunning and thought-provoking. The idea of spirit lines is a beautiful way of describing connections that are not seen, but exist and can be felt. This idea is going to stay with me; I can see how it will continue to teach me and remind me of spiritual aspects and connections that are so important, but not necessarily valued within settler colonial school systems. I admire how Peatr sought out more information about spirit lines before depicting them in his own practice. In his inquiry about spirit lines, he modelled how to draw inspiration, find deeper meaning, and learn about their purposes and origin, using them only after really understanding their significance.

EDUCATOR INQUIRY AND ACTIONS

- Research pictographs, petroglyphs, or petroforms in your area.[3] As a school team, discuss the considerations and logistics for taking students or teachers to visit the site. Write a grant proposal to acquire funding to do so.

- Research efforts that have been made to protect and interpret pictograph or petroglyph sites in your region. How can you support initiatives that aim to safeguard these cultural treasures for future generations?

- Think about how your school team approaches the curriculum of teaching ancient civilizations. For example, how has imagery from faraway places been prioritized over local imagery?

---

3   The podcast *Arch365* offers an excellent explanation of the differences between petroglyphs and pictographs; see Episode 136, "Petroglyphs and Pictographs," hosted by Chris Webster, May 16, 2017, www.archaeologypodcastnetwork.com/arch365/136.

- In your role as an educator, where do you see yourself fitting into the continuation of cultural transmission?[4] Whose culture are you transmitting and to whom? What questions, tensions, and synergies exist? Challenge yourself to represent this in a visual format.

- Think about the concept of connecting lines in relation to your professional practice. What ideas would be joined by emotional or spiritual connections? What does this type of thinking reveal?

Classroom Connections

Introduce to students the artwork and narrative and the Connected Concepts you wish to focus on. Use the following questions, prompts, and resource suggestions to guide student learning.

CONNECTED CONCEPTS
- Pictographs
- Oral and visual transmission of culture
- Land and water dwellers

CONNECTING TO SELF: PROMPTS FOR PERSONAL REFLECTION
⟩ **Beginning**
- What animals or beings do you know of that represent generational knowledges in your culture? What animal or beings understand the worlds of both land and water?

- Reflect on the presence of visual imagery in your daily life, such as images on social media or websites. What have you learned from these images?

---

4   *Cultural transmission* refers to the ways in which various elements of culture, including language, practices, and spirituality, are passed down to future generations.

❯ Bridging

- If you were to draw lines to connect two images, what images would you choose and why?

- When have you played a role in cultural preservation or transmission?

● Beyond

- Have you ever encountered rock carvings, pictographs, petroglyphs, or other ancient art? How do you think these artistic expressions contribute to preserving and sharing cultural stories over time?

- Reflect on the role of art and storytelling in maintaining cultural identity.

CONNECTING TO COMMUNITY: PROMPTS FOR LEARNING CIRCLES

❯ Beginning

- Discuss why visual imagery is so powerful and long-lasting.

- Share an image from your past that continues to speak to you.

❯ Bridging

- Discuss your ideas about the messages that Sturgeon might tell Turtle.

- Imagine you are creating a pictograph or petroglyph. Share the story or message you would paint or carve to pass on to future generations.

● Beyond

- Share your interpretation of what it means to "understand both worlds" (land and water) for Turtle and for yourself.

- Share a memory of a time when you learned something important through a story or visual representation. How did the way the information was presented impact your understanding of the subject?

- Share your favorite meme and analyze the underlying social commentary it offers. Consider how this commentary aligns or contrasts with the messages conveyed through Indigenous pictographs and petroglyphs, which are rich in cultural significance and often hold deep connections to the land and community.

CONNECTING TO LAND-BASED LEARNING

❭ Beginning

- Are there pictographs, petroglyphs, or petroforms in your local area? If so, think about how you could plan a trip to see them.

- Locate Peatr Thomas's mother's home territory of Bloodvein First Nation on a map. What can you find out about the community, including the agreements made on the land? Find out more about the pictographs in Bloodvein, Manitoba, using resources such as the Pimachiowin Aki website <pimaki.ca/5-spectacular-pictographs-explained/>, or by connecting to a local Knowledge Keeper, art historian, or curator.

❭ Bridging

- As a class, take a walking tour to view street art in your community. What do you see? Who might have created this artwork and why? Compare and contrast the words and images in the street art to Peatr's artwork.

- Compare and contrast cultural groups that have used visual imagery similar to pictographs or petroglyphs. What knowledges are held within both the process and product of these visuals?

● Beyond

- Research another place where culture is transmitted through oral or visual means. What is the message or knowledge that is shared, and does it connect to the message you think is shared in Peatr Thomas's work? If so, how?

- Are there examples of Indigenous artwork in your school or community? What are the mediums or the messages of these works in relation to land? View this artwork and discuss with your classmates how it transmits cultural knowledge to viewers.

CONNECTING TO LAND BACK

- Find out more about how to access the pictographs along the Bloodvein River that Peatr Thomas describes, or other pictographs, petroglyphs, and petroforms. Have they been preserved? If so, how? Who currently has access to them? Who is responsible for acting as a caretaker for them? If you notice disconnections between the original creators of the pictographs, petroglyphs, and petroforms and future generations, how might you support their preservation?

- Bloodvein River First Nation is in Treaty 5 territory. The peoples of Treaty 5 received "a one-time payment of $5 upon signing the treaty, instead of the $12 given to the peoples of Treaties 3 and 4, and... one-quarter of the land."[5] *Pimitotah: To Care for Our Land*, a land use plan created by the Bloodvein River First Nation and the Government of Manitoba, outlines the community's self-initiated land protection projects.[6] The document focuses on upholding "the land for future generations of Anishinabe people, wildlife and other living things."[7] It further states, "As people who use the land for livelihood purposes, we view the land and all its contents as a necessity. Everything taken has a purpose and is to be respected at all times. Nothing is wasted."[8] Read the vision statement on page 6. Using it as inspiration, write your own vision statement that reflects your feelings on how the land where you live should be cared for.

CONNECTING TO OTHER INDIGENOUS RESOURCES

Books

Manitowapow: Aboriginal Writings from the Land of Water, edited by Niigaan-wewidam James Sinclair and Warren Cariou (HighWater Press, 2012). This collection of Indigenous voices helps readers get to know the place now known as Manitoba. The introduction provides information about Indigenous writing systems and the significance and meanings behind petroforms.

---

5   Michelle Filice, "Treaty 5," The Canadian Encyclopedia, www.thecanadianencyclopedia.ca/en /article/treaty-5.

6   Bloodvein First Nation and Manitoba Planning Team, *Pimitotah: To Care for Our Land—Bloodvein First Nation Land Use Plan* (2014), pimaki.ca/wp-content/uploads/Bloodvein-First-Nation-Land-Use-Plan.pdf.

7   Bloodvein First Nation and Manitoba Planning Team, *Pimitotah*, 8.

8   Bloodvein First Nation and Manitoba Planning Team, *Pimitotah*, 17.

Kinikinik: A Treaty Play, by Ian Ross (Treaty Relations Commission of Manitoba, 2010). <education.afn.ca/afntoolkit/wp-content/uploads/2021 /04/Kinikinik-playbill_042810_SCREEN_singles.pdf>.
This reader's theatre play, which helps teach about treaties and respectful relationships, features a conversation between a turtle, wolf, and beaver. It can be read and performed for a variety of ages.

Online

"5 Spectacular Pictographs Explained," Pimachiowin Aki World Heritage Site, June 15, 2020. <pimaki.ca/5-spectacular-pictographs-explained/>.
This comprehensive website shares valuable information about Pimachiowin Aki, the first World Heritage site in Manitoba, and about guardianship and the protection and preservation of cultural heritage.

Images on Stone: A Virtual Exhibition on Rock Art in Canada, Museum of Civilization. <imagesdanslapierre.mcq.org/en/>.
This site documents petroglyphs at five national historic sites in Canada, including cultural affiliations, translations of Indigenous place names, photographs, and videos of Indigenous people describing the cultural significance of the sites. It offers a great entry point for students of all ages.

Marianne Nicolson, The Medicine Project. <themedicineproject.com /marianne-nicolson.html>.
This site describes the work of artist Marianne Nicolson (Kwakwa̱ka̱'wakw First Nation), who creates large-scale rock and cliff paintings in Kwakwa̱ka̱'wakw style. While her art differs from Peatr Thomas's style and traditions, it shows the diversity among pictograph styles.

Pimitotah: To Care for Our Land—Bloodvein First Nation Land Use Plan, Bloodvein First Nation and Manitoba Planning Team (Revised September 25, 2014). <www.gov.mb.ca/nrnd/forest/pubs/forest_lands/land/bloodvein _land_use_plan_revised.pdf>.
This document provides details of the Bloodvein First Nation's plan to protect and manage its lands according to Anishinaabe values and management systems and Western scientific knowledge.

Homelands and Waterways

TYNA LEGAULT TAYLOR, a member of Attawapiskat First Nation, is a writer, scholar, and advocate for Indigenous food and water sovereignty. She learned her Omushkego Cree culture through teachings and water- and land-based food practices passed down by her late mother and kokum, despite colonial interference to deskill Indigenous knowledge systems. Tyna is currently pursuing her PhD in Health Sciences at Lakehead University, where her research focuses on water justice and sovereignty in First Nations communities.

FIRST, I WANT YOU TO IMAGINE being told *not* to wash your food with the water in your home, and *not* to use your shower for more than five minutes. I want you to imagine being told *not* to boil the water, because doing so will concentrate chemicals that can evaporate into the air you are breathing. The community of Attawapiskat First Nation, like many other Indigenous communities across Canada, has been living with this reality for decades. They do not need to imagine.

Attawapiskat First Nation—also known as Kattawapiskak in Cree, meaning "people of the parting rocks"—is a remote coastal community located on the Traditional Territory of the Omushkego (Swampy Cree) James Bay Cree of Treaty 9, located between the Canadian Shield and James Bay and Hudson Bay. Timmins, Ontario, is the nearest urban centre, located approximately 500 kilometres to the south. Attawapiskat First Nation is a fly-in community that can be accessed by a winter road from January to March, linking it to Fort Albany, Kashechewan, Moosonee, Moose Factory, and Timmins.

As an Omushkego Cree woman and member of Attawapiskat First Nation, I had the opportunity to reconnect and "re-search" back[1] on my own community and ancestral homelands and waterways through a research project I undertook while completing my master of arts degree at Lakehead University. The project aimed to create awareness and dialogue about food justice, food insecurity, Indigenous food sovereignty, and ongoing healing in Attawapiskat First Nation. However, in listening to the voices and living stories of the people of Attawapiskat, it became clear to me that water justice and water sovereignty must be enacted for food justice and Indigenous food sovereignty to be supported.

Indigenous Peoples rely on waterways as the lifeblood of their homelands, whether for drinking, bathing, cooking, ceremonies, and transportation, or in keeping the land, plants, animals, and aquatic life healthy for future generations. Land and water are central to retaining and revitalizing Indigenous languages, and to re-learning culture through water- and land-based activities with family and community. Without land and water, Indigenous ways of life will cease to exist.

Attawapiskat has fourth-world socio-economic conditions, including no potable water; expensive market food, gas, water, equipment, and supplies for water- and land-based food practices; a housing and infrastructure crisis; and high suicide rates.[2] *Fourth world* is a term coined by the late Secwépemc Chief George Manuel to refer to third-world conditions or realities that exist within a first-world country such as Canada.[3]

1　Kathleen E. Absolon, *Kaandossiwin: How We Come to Know: Indigenous Re-Search Methodologies*, 2nd ed. (Fernwood Publishing, 2022).

2　Dawn Morrison, "Reflections and Realities: Expressions of Food Sovereignty in the Fourth World," in *Indigenous Food Systems: Concepts, Cases, and Conversations*, ed. Priscilla Settee and Shilesh Shukla (Women's Press, 2020), 17; Ian Austen, "Suicides Plague Attawapiskat First Nation in Canada," *New York Times*, April 12, 2016.

3　George Manuel and Michael Posluns, *The Fourth World: An Indian Reality* (University of Minnesota Press, 1974).

The legacy of settler colonialism has contributed to the water crisis by limiting the capacities of First Nations peoples.[4] Strategically, the Canadian government used settler colonial policies to relocate First Nations peoples to reserves through the negotiation of the treaties that subsequently confined them to these lands.[5] Here, food insecurity and unsafe water emerged, creating a dependency on the government.[6]

First Nations peoples, including members of Attawapiskat, are still feeling the effects of governments that produce vulnerable peoples, "increasing the risk of death" through the lack of basic needs such as safe drinking water, access to land for Indigenous foods and food practices, and affordable market foods.[7] Environmental stewardship and connection to the natural world has been disrupted though dispossession of lands, ultimately disempowering Indigenous Peoples' way of life.[8]

Yet, through "survivance,"[9] which goes beyond resistance and survival, Indigenous Peoples are transitioning back to thriving communities at their own pace of recovery. In Attawapiskat, community members continue to speak their Cree language, practise their traditional Cree culture (including the spring goose hunt on Akimiski Island), and hunt, fish, and gather along the Attawapiskat River using their traditional land use and travel ways.

---

4   Settler colonialism is a distinct form of colonialism that aims to create a permanent settlement, claiming stolen lands and resources with the goal of creating a new national settler identity while erasing the identity of Indigenous peoples; see Lana Ray, Kristin Burnett, and Catherine Sergerie, "Examining Indigenous Food Sovereignty as a Conceptual Framework for Health in Two Urban Communities in Northern Ontario, Canada," *Global Health Promotion* 26, Suppl. 3 (2019): 54–63.

5   Ray et al., "Examining Indigenous Food Sovereignty."

6   Jerry P. White, Laura Murphy, and Nicholas Spence, "Water and Indigenous Peoples: Canada's Paradox," *International Indigenous Policy Journal* 3, no. 3 (2012): 1–25.

7   Julie Guthman, "Doing Justice to Bodies? Reflections on Food Justice, Race, and Biology," *Antipode* 46, no. 5 (2012): 1154–71.

8   Charlotte Reading and Fred Wien, *Health Inequalities and Social Determinants of Aboriginal Peoples' Health* (National Collaborating Centre for Aboriginal Health, 2009); Ray et al., "Examining Indigenous Food Sovereignty."

9   Survivance is not merely a reaction or surviving, it's taking action. It is the continuance and revival of Indigenous knowledge, stories, language, and connection to land, water, and all living beings, with the aim to thrive as Indigenous communities and nations; see Gerald Robert Vizenor, *Manifest Manners: Postindian Warriors of Survivance* (Wesleyan University Press, 1994). My re-search was an act of survivance enacted by re-connecting with land, Cree food knowledge and land-based practices, and community, and by sharing our stories of resurgence along with our hope and vision for future generations; see Eve Tuck, "Suspending Damage: A Letter to Communities," *Harvard Educational Review* 79, no. 3 (2009): 409–28.

These water- and land-based food practices are central to the identity and culture of the Cree Peoples of Attawapiskat. However, there are ongoing concerns about environmental impacts on their homelands and waterways.

Federal and provincial government–approved exploitation of lands and extraction of resources, such as the De Beers Victor diamond mine located 90 kilometres west of Attawapiskat, continues to have long-term environmental consequences, including mercury contamination of waterways.[10] Mercury contamination has contributed to the decline in traditional harvesting of fish, as community members are advised to eat only one fish per month. In addition, Knowledge Keepers and hunters/trappers remind us that future mining developments hold potential risk for further contamination of homelands and waterways, producing further colonial disruptions to food and water justice in Attawapiskat and the Traditional Territory of Treaty 9.

In many cases, governments have failed to consult with Indigenous communities in making crucial decisions about land and water. Water infrastructure and design initiatives must be specific to the individual community, reflecting its geographic surroundings and integrating traditional beliefs and principles of respecting water. They must acknowledge water's spiritual nature, and how it is alive. Imposed water treatment options, such as reverse osmosis in Attawapiskat, remove everything from the water, including the spirit. Other options, such as slow sand filtration—which is used in Curve Lake First Nation—imitate a more natural process to ensure the water is treated with respect. Elders and other members from Attawapiskat have reverted to how they got water growing up: drawing it from the river in the spring, and from snow and chopped ice in the winter. They believe it to be more alive than the dead water provided at the two watering stations that rely on reverse osmosis.

Indigenous communities must have self-determination and autonomy in developing their own paths toward water sovereignty and water justice. Transformative change should be Indigenous- and community-led, with allies working with Indigenous communities rather than making decisions in their "best interests," which could lead to power imbalances and

---

10 "De Beers Pleads Guilty to Failing to Report Mercury Monitoring Data Near Northern Ontario Mine," CBC News, July 6, 2021, www.cbc.ca/news/canada/sudbury/debeers-court-timmins-mercury-pollution-case-1.6091664.

reinforce "problematic patterns of exploitation, domination, and dependency."[11] It is important to centre the voices of Indigenous Peoples who have the expertise to identify and address their water challenges.[12] This includes listening to the living water stories and Traditional Ecological Knowledge that Indigenous Peoples hold. In Attawapiskat, community members have been conducting their own research using their Traditional Ecological Knowledge to observe changes to the land and waterways. They have studied the impacts of the De Beers Victor diamond mine and how future mining developments, such as the Ring of Fire, will impact the land and waterways. Knowledge Keepers of Attawapiskat are creating awareness about how the rivers surrounding the Ring of Fire, including the Muketei River, join with the Attawapiskat River. Any contamination from the mine will flow down the Attawapiskat River to various waterways, such as the Ekwan River watershed, further impacting the community's drinking water, aquatic life, and animals.

Although hope and vision are important, they must be followed up with community commitment, solidarity, and action. These acts involve "sacrifice, persistence, patience, and a slow, painful movement,"[13] something the community of Attawapiskat and many other Indigenous communities across Canada know all too well. Vision also requires leadership skills that inspire, unite, and create hope for a sustainable future—one that includes justice through clean, safe drinking and bathing water. Ongoing initiatives that respect traditional Cree water- and land-based knowledge and practices are working to bring awareness to members of Attawapiskat and surrounding Omushkego communities and allies, to seek their support for the hope and vision of defending and protecting homelands and waterways for future generations.

---

11 Valentine K. Cadieux and Rachel Slocum, "What Does It Mean to Do Food Justice?" *Journal of Political Ecology* 22, no. 1 (2015): 1–26.

12 Barbara Parker, "Exploring Intersectional Feminist Food Pedagogies Through the Recipe Exchange Project," in *Food Futures in Education and Society*, ed. Gurpinder Lalli, Angela Turner, and Marion Rutland (Routledge, 2023); Lauren Kepkiewcz et al., "Beyond Inclusion: Toward an Anti-Colonial Food Justice Praxis," *Journal of Agriculture, Food Systems, and Community Development* 5, no. 4 (2015): 99–104.

13 Leanne Simpson, *Dancing on Our Turtle's Back: Stories of Nishnaabeg Re-Creation, Resurgence, and a New Emergence* (ARP Books, 2011), 67.

Educator Connections

Read the editors' thoughts and engage in reflection. Respond to the questions that follow on your own or with your colleague(s).

PERSONAL CONNECTIONS

Christine: Reading Tyna Legault Taylor's essay and learning about the reality of life for people living in Attawapiskat is hard. As someone who was raised in the city, I can't imagine life without clean water. My urban upbringing shielded me from the harsh realities many Indigenous communities face daily. I've taken for granted amenities like clean water without truly comprehending the privilege they represent. Tyna's essay is a poignant reminder that there is so much more we need to understand, acknowledge, and act upon. As someone from the city, it's my responsibility to be more informed, to advocate for equity, and to support efforts that combat environmental racism.

Katya: The realities of Canada as a fourth-world country are appalling and frightening. My dad used to stress the importance of taking care of the waters in Manitoba. He always said that many people value gold, but there will come a time when people realize that water is more valuable than gold. What a privilege it is to have clean water in Winnipeg—water that was unjustly taken through an aqueduct from Shoal Lake 40 First Nation.[14] Tyna Legault Taylor's essay reveals such a clear example of settler colonialism: communities don't have access to safe water, and settlers and colonial systems have made this the reality. A few years ago, we went without water for a few days because of an issue with old pipes in the area where I live in Winnipeg. People were very upset by this brief period without water, yet reserve communities like Attawapiskat have thirsted for far too long. Do I respect the water I drink, wash dishes with, and bath my kids in? How can I teach my children more sustainable ways?

---

14 For an analysis of the development of Winnipeg's water supply as an example of settler colonialism, see Adele Perry, *Aqueduct: Colonialism, Resources, and the Histories We Remember* (ARP Books, 2016).

- Think about the ways in which access to water is monitored within the school building. Do all kids have access to clean water? Are sustainability measures taken? How so?

- Take an inventory of the ways water is used in the school. Look for areas that can be improved and water-saving measures that can be taken, such as flow-limiting faucets. Could water be recycled for some purposes?

- Think about the term *settler colonialism* and discuss how living in a settler colonial state affects your role and responsibilities as a citizen in Canada.

- Tyna Legault Taylor shares that before food sovereignty can be fully confronted, water justice must be addressed. Discuss why this is and consider how these two issues are integrally connected.

- Learn about the food and water insecurity that exists in your school community, city, province, territory, or nation. Find a person who can act as a connection to learning more. How can the school embody a solution to this issue?

- Consider what steps property owners or renters can take to reconcile Indigenous land-dispossession history and fulfill their environmental responsibility when residing on or using traditional Indigenous territory.

- Work with students to form a land and water defenders' group that meets regularly to discuss how to protect homelands and waterways for future generations.

Classroom Connections

Introduce to students the narrative and the Connected Concepts you wish to focus on. Use the following questions, prompts, and resource suggestions to guide student learning.

CONNECTED CONCEPTS

- Water justice/water and food sovereignty
- Environmental racism
- Survivance

CONNECTING TO SELF: PROMPTS FOR PERSONAL REFLECTION

❯ Beginning

- List all the moments in a typical day when you use water. How important is water in your daily life?

- How can you show gratitude toward water?

- How do animals use water? What can we learn from them?

❯ Bridging

- What does water justice mean to you?

- Think about a popular water source near you. Who has access to this water? Who is responsible for caring for this water?

- How can we protect the land and water?

● Beyond

- How can you use your agency to advance water justice in your community, province, or nation?

- What are examples of "fourth-world socio-economic conditions" in your local territories?

CONNECTING TO COMMUNITY: PROMPTS FOR LEARNING CIRCLES

❯ Beginning

- Share one reason why you are thankful for water. Try to think of a reason that hasn't been said yet.

- Share your favourite land-based activity. How might this activity be affected by climate change or other environmental changes?

- Dive into your favourite memories of water. Share why these memories are special to you.

❯ Bridging

- Discuss cultural practices involving water in your ancestral traditions.

- Discuss how your family or community traditionally collects, uses, or celebrates water, including how this practice has changed over time.

- Share a story or learning experience that connects to water.

● Beyond

- Discuss your understandings of the terms *food sovereignty* and *water justice*. Share some of your own connections to these terms. For example, how do some of the foods you eat contribute to excessive use of water?

- Discuss the concept of "fourth-world socio-economic conditions."

- Discuss how changes to Earth's climate and increasingly unpredictable weather patterns will affect access to water and access on water and ice to and from communities, and the subsequent impact on food sovereignty.

CONNECTING TO LAND-BASED LEARNING

❯ Beginning

- Locate Attawapiskat First Nation on a map. What can you find out about the community, including treaties or land agreements?

- Learn about an aspect of Traditional Ecological Knowledge from an Elder, Knowledge Keeper, or Indigenous community member in your local area. What do they and their community know about their environment? How did they come to know this? What values might this knowledge promote?

- Find a way to reduce your negative impact on the Earth. For example, to reduce waste, put together a set of reusable dishes and cutlery (sometimes referred to as a "feast bundle" in Indigenous communities) that can be used when eating outside, at work, or at gatherings. Collect a cup, bowl, plate, cloth napkin, and reusable utensils in a cloth bag.

- Look at water cycles and find animals whose life cycles interconnect with and depend on these cycles.

▶ Bridging

- Find out more about where your water is sourced from. Which bodies of water does your drinking water come from and what path does it take to get to you? Which direction does it flow? Research, look at maps, and ask people for help with finding more information. Represent your findings in a "flow" chart. Consider the similarities and differences between modern water management practices and local Indigenous principles.

- Take action to advocate for Attawapiskat and the many other Indigenous communities without clean drinking water; for example, write a letter, create a social media campaign, or set up a fundraiser.

● Beyond

- Find a body of water or waterway where you live. Walk along its banks. What did you encounter along this journey? What evidence do you see that indicates if it is a healthy ecosystem?

- Research Indigenous communities that don't have access to clean drinking water. Find information about how long this has been the case, who is responsible for creating the problem and for solving it, and what possible solutions there are to the problem.

- Learn about an Indigenous creation story, oral tradition, or cultural practice that emphasizes the significance of water. Reflect on how these teachings shape perspectives on the environment and the responsibility to protect water. Think about water as sacred versus water as a resource or commodity.

CONNECTING TO LAND BACK

- Attawapiskat is clear example of the disastrous effects of settler colonialism on land and water. While the community is connected by proximity to water, it has become disconnected from water because the water that is supposed to be healing is now harmful. This has been described as a humanitarian crisis. How can we re-instill a respect for water in ourselves?

- The commodification and extraction of diamonds affected the sustainability of the water in Attawapiskat First Nation. Tyna Legault Taylor discusses government failure "in not consulting with Indigenous communities in making crucial decisions about land and water." Research other communities affected by mining, mercury contamination, and the poisoning of water and fish populations, such as Grassy Narrows First Nation, which sued the Ontario provincial and federal governments in 2024. What solutions to these issues have been proposed by the affected communities and how might you support their efforts?

CONNECTIONS TO OTHER INDIGENOUS RESOURCES

Books

We Are Water Protectors, by Carole Lindstrom (Roaring Brook Press, 2020; ages 3–6).
This award-winning picture book encourages readers to think about ways to protect water and become activists.

Dipnetting with Dad, by Willie Sellars (Caitlin Press, 2014; ages 4–7).
This picture book tells the story of a boy going dipnetting with his dad, catching his first salmon, and preparing, drying, and cooking it.

Autumn Peltier, Water Warrior, by Carole Lindstrom (Roaring Brook Press, 2023; ages 4–8).
This picture book shares the story of two generations of Water Walkers: Autumn Peltier and her great-aunt Josephine Mandamin. Includes a glossary and information about Autumn Peltier.

Dad, Is It Time to Gather Mint?, by Tyna Legault Taylor (HighWater Press, 2025; ages 5–8).
This picture book (featuring both the Omushkegomowin and Anishinaabemowin languages) describes the traditional activities on the land that a boy does with his dad throughout the seasons.

River Woman, by katherena vermette (House of Anansi Press, 2018).
This book of poetry explores love as a decolonial action. The poems are grounded in the continuous relationship between land, water, and identity.

Films

Life in the City of Dirty Water, directed by Clayton Thomas-Müller (CBC Docs, 2020). <www.youtube.com/watch?v=ANw8XmNkbCM>.
This short documentary shares Cree activist Clayton Thomas-Müller's personal journey of trauma, healing, and renewal. It describes his roles in Indigenous-led environmental protection initiatives. This documentary contains mature content.

The People of the Kattawapiskak River, directed by Alanis Obomsawin (National Film Board, 2012). <www.nfb.ca/film/people_of_kattawapiskak_river/>.
This documentary focuses on the impoverished living conditions on Attawapiskat First Nation.

Online

Neskantaga First Nation. <neskantaga.com/>.
This website includes videos sharing voices from members of the remote Ojibwe community of Neskantaga First Nation, which is under a long-standing boil-water advisory. The homepage provides an ongoing count of the days the community has been under the advisory.

"Sacred Value of Water," Indigenous Climate Action.
<www.indigenousclimateaction.com/entries/sacred-value-of-water>.
This website shares the vision and work of Indigenous Climate Action to "inspire action through the development of tools and opportunities created with, by, and for our communities, with the goal of uplifting Indigenous voices, sovereignty, and stewardship of the lands and waters for future generations." Includes blog entries, media releases, and ways to take action.

PART TWO

BEING

THIS SECTION encourages renewed ways of *being* on the land. It aims to activate new pathways for land-based education by merging ancestral and contemporary expressions. The contributors inspire us to go beyond written text and linear learning to begin thinking about cycles and generations. The works featured here highlight many entry points to land-based education: through time spent in the forest, through the lens of a camera, and through digital spaces. They share practical and pragmatic connections that show us how being in relationship with land teaches us survival skills and about our own character and values.

Ways of being in connection to land are shared in the poetry of Shannon Webb-Campbell (Mi'kmaq), the writing of Dr. Tasha Beeds (of nêhiyaw, Scottish-Métis, and Bajan ancestry), the art of Sonny Assu (Ligwiłda'xw of the Kwakw<u>a</u>ka'wakw Nations), and the photographs taken by Inuit students from Jonah Amitnaaq Secondary School in Qamani'tuaq (ᖃᒪᓂᑦᐊᖅ), or Baker Lake, Nunavut.

Activating and defending are two actions and ways of being that stand out as a focus of these contributors. In her powerful essay, Dr. Tasha Beeds introduces the verb *activate*, which brings to life the power of Indigeneity. She invites readers to consider what it means to be Indigenous, and encourages settler educators to move beyond the classroom, to "step up to educate their own people and address negative behaviour" (page 101). This idea of stepping up is a way of being that adopts an active learning stance, taking a stand in opposition to the status quo or settler colonialism. As you read, be attuned to emotional connections and visceral responses "activated" within your being.

This section gives guidance to settler educators for how to activate land-based teaching and learning. The trips taken by students from Jonah Amitnaaq Secondary School prioritize land-based experiences in partnership with local Knowledge Keepers and create an opportunity for non-Indigenous teachers to learn alongside and from students and community members as they practise Inuit cultural traditions. Viewing the photographs taken by the students on the land allows us to see through their eyes (and lenses) and prompts us to think of education that goes beyond the classroom. It is valuable and possible!

Ideas of being reverent of the sacred ecology of land, viewing the land as a kinship relationship, and defending the land are shared in Shannon Webb-Campbell's poem and Sonny Assu's artworks. Webb-Campbell takes us on a lyrical journey into being in the boreal forest among strong, trembling trees. Each word hangs like a leaf on a branch, its placement intentional and given much nurturing and support. Webb-Campbell's words prompt us to consider what might be different if we sought new ways of being in relationship to land and each other. What would be different if we prioritized and defended the health of the land and people over individual quests for land and wealth?

Inspired by Wet'suwet'en land defenders, Assu's work encourages us to be curious about how we think (or don't think) about land. While digital imagery may seem far from land-based education, a deep dive into the layers of expression and meaning in Assu's work shows how his imagery transcends time and place. It is deeply rooted in his ancestral traditions, conveying visual symbolism that has been tied to the land for generations.

As you enter this section, consider the following: What new ways of being are important for future generations? How can you thoughtfully take steps to defend the land? How can you take care to act "as though the ancestors are watching"?

CONNECTING ONLINE

Post reflections from your own learning or share how you take up these ideas in your educational setting using the hashtags #FootbridgeRenewalBook and #FootbridgeRenewal.

"Ecology of Being"

SHANNON WEBB-CAMPBELL is a critic, poet, and writer of Mi'kmaq and settler heritage. She is the author of *Still No Word* (2015), which received Egale Canada's Out in Print Award, and *I Am a Body of Land* (2019). Shannon is pursuing her PhD at the University of New Brunswick in the Department of English. She is a member of Qalipu Mi'kmaq First Nation and lives in Kjipuktuk/Halifax in Mi'kma'ki.

––––––––

Ecology of Being[1]

in this thinner air
there is no need to *ingest crystals*
we are surrounded by the boreal forest
at the breakdown of natural order
within the great chain of chaos
we exist as intervention
between land and sky
only to return from a journey
to a place of familiarization
forgo the power of selfhood
pain is singular—
it triggers memorable experiences
if you embody new occult poetics
between the self and this other thing
we make a clearing to find meaning
travel to trembling aspens
and come upon medicines
we remember this leaf
make connections
experience seasons at their breaking point
and reinvent our skin cells

1   "Ecology of Being" from *Lunar Tides* © 2021 by Shannon Webb-Campbell. Used with permission of Book*hug Press.

Educator Connections

Read the editors' thoughts and engage in reflection. Respond to the questions that follow on your own or with your colleague(s).

PERSONAL CONNECTIONS

Christine: After reading Shannon Webb-Campbell's poem, I had to sit back and take in the deeper meaning. It has me thinking about the purpose of life, the place our consciousness goes when we die, and enjoying the journey along the way. The line "forgo the power of self-hood" stands out to me because lately I've been thinking about how we live in a society that values individualism over the collective, which differs from traditional Indigenous values of community and connectedness. As an educator, I'm thinking of ways we can teach youth to think about community more. Perhaps by reconnecting with the land around us, we can rediscover our connection to each other as well.

Katya: I have been carrying Shannon Webb-Campbell's poem around with me as I drive, walk, and work. These lines stand out to me: "we exist as intervention / between land and sky / only to return from a journey / to a place of familiarization." I think about what is natural and what is familiar. How have I become so comfortable in what is unnatural, in what is not meant to be here but is so familiar that I have taken it for granted? My sense of direction is guided more by the streets than by where the river winds. Have I been blinded by a lifestyle that does not do enough to honour and revere natural elements that are familiar? As I drive down a major road in Winnipeg that was recently renamed Abinojii Mikanah (meaning "Children's Way"), I try to block out what is made by humans and focus on the types of trees that line the roads, where the nests are, and which birds live there. I notice nature persisting and resisting the unnatural human creations that continue to push nature to its limits. If humans let nature take over for a week, a month, a year, or more, what might we learn?

- What do you think is signified by the poem's depiction of human existence as an intervention between land and sky? How might this impact our understanding of Indigenous relationships with nature and the environment?

- What lessons from the forest could be implemented in your workplace or educational setting?

- Has this poem shifted your perspective of human experiences in the natural world, particularly in the context of the boreal forest? If so, how?

- In the context of modern society and Western cultural perspectives, consider some obstacles to achieving the balance and harmony with nature alluded to in the poem.

- As a school team, organize a walk or field trip to an accessible urban location where the group can observe and reflect on ecological connections. Encourage team members to make connections between their observations and the themes of the poem.

- Reflect on the following lines from "Ecology of Being" in relation to your own teaching: "forgo the power of selfhood / pain is singular." How might this perspective on selfhood and pain influence the way you approach discussions about nature, healing, and interconnectedness with your students?

Classroom Connections

Introduce to students the poem and the Connected Concepts you wish to focus on. Use the following questions, prompts, and resource suggestions to guide student learning.

- Selfhood
- Interconnectedness
- Medicine

CONNECTING TO SELF: PROMPTS FOR PERSONAL REFLECTION

⟩ Beginning

- "Ecology of Being" refers to "seasons at their breaking point." What is your favourite season and why?

- If you were a tree, what season do you think you would like the most? Why?

⟩ Bridging

- Start a nature journal and go on regular walks. Record your observations, thoughts, and reflections on the changing seasons. What do you notice about the interconnectedness of nature?

- How does the poem highlight the role of nature in healing and understanding? Can you think of any personal experiences or stories where nature played a role of healing or understanding in your life?

● Beyond

- Reflect on the following lines: "we exist as intervention / between land and sky." What do you think this says about the role of human beings in nature and our connection to nature? How might these lines connect to Indigenous ways of knowing and being?

- Reflect on the poem's closing line: "and reinvent our skin cells." How does nature inspire or influence personal growth, renewal, or change for you?

CONNECTING TO COMMUNITY: PROMPTS FOR LEARNING CIRCLES

⟩ Beginning

- Describe your feelings or reactions when the seasons change. Share specific natural occurrences in relation to seasonal changes that you appreciate.

- Share your favourite line from "Ecology of Being" and describe why it spoke to you.

⟩ Bridging

- The poem includes the line, "we make a clearing to find meaning." Describe a time when you had to clear your mind to understand something better and how this helped you.

- Share words or imagery from the poem that you connect to or think are interesting or important. Explain why you chose these words or images.

● **Beyond**
  - Consider the Indigenous perspective presented in the poem and how it compares to Western views on nature and selfhood.

  - Elaborate on how spending time in nature or on the land encourages people to "forgo the power of selfhood."

CONNECTING TO LAND-BASED LEARNING

❱ **Beginning**
  - Venture outside to collect different types of leaves. Discuss their shapes, colours, and textures. Use the leaves to create a collaborative art piece on a specific topic or one of the Connected Concepts.

  - Create a list of items mentioned in "Ecology of Being" (e.g., leaves, berries, aspen trees). Find and observe these items in nature.

❱ **Bridging**
  - Find a spot outside where you can sit quietly. Reflect on and find personal meaning in the ecology of that place.

  - Create a school garden. Learn about growth cycles of plants and how they can be nurtured to thrive, just as the writer alludes to the growth of plants in the poem.

  - Learn basic photography skills and create a photo story that showcases the beauty you witness in the natural world.

● **Beyond**
  - Go on a walk with an Indigenous Knowledge Keeper to identify and discuss different local plants, especially any medicinal or cultural significance they might have.

- Research the medicinal uses of trembling aspen as described in the poem. Learn more about Indigenous healing practices and their significance in culture and nature, and discuss the importance of preserving and respecting these traditions.

- Map or draw how various cultures have articulated the seasons and natural cycles of nature.

CONNECTING TO LAND BACK

- Colonialism continues to impact the "ecology of being" and the interconnectedness of beings. In this poem, Shannon Webb-Campbell writes about the tension resulting from "the breakdown of natural order." How has settler colonialism intervened against the natural order of things?

- The poem underscores the interconnectedness of Indigenous communities and the natural environment. Within the Land Back movement, land is recognized not just as a physical resource, but also as a vital aspect of Indigenous culture, spirituality, and identity. The poem's depiction of humans as interventions between land and sky reflects the Indigenous perspective that our existence is intricately linked with the land, reinforcing the significance of land as part of our identity. What types of ecological relationships might be restored by giving land back? What aspects of ourselves might this process require us to give back or give up?

CONNECTIONS TO OTHER INDIGENOUS RESOURCES

Books

We Dream Medicine Dreams, by Lisa Boivin (HighWater Press, 2021; ages 6–8). A healing story about life, death, grief, and Indigenous (Dene) teachings, connections to animals, and intergenerational knowledge, with striking digital imagery on a black background to represent the dark history of colonialism.

Siha Tooskin Knows series, by Charlene and Wilson Bearhead (HighWater Press, 2020; ages 9–12).
This series focuses on the life of an 11-year-old Nakota boy who learns about aspects of his culture and the gifts of his people from his family members. In particular, *Siha Tooskin Knows the Nature of Life*, *Siha Tooskin Knows the Best Medicine*, and *Siha Tooskin Knows the Offering of Tobacco* explore themes relevant to this poem.

Braiding Sweetgrass for Young Adults: Indigenous Wisdom, Scientific Knowledge, and the Teachings of Plants, by Robin Wall Kimmerer, adapted by Monique Gray Smith (Zest Books, 2022; ages 12–18).
This text shares Indigenous knowledges braided into narratives from the perspective of a botanist from Potawatomi Nation. It shares Indigenous wisdom while also teaching about plants and the interconnections within ecosystems. This version includes informational sidebars, reflection questions, and additional art.

Held by the Land: A Guide to Indigenous Plants for Wellness, by Leigh Joseph (Wellfleet Press, 2023).
Joseph, an ethnobotanist and member of Squamish Nation, provides a beautifully illustrated introduction to Indigenous plant knowledge.

Medicine Walk, by Richard Wagamese (McClelland & Stewart, 2015).
This adult novel is about a young man called to journey to his dad's side as he is dying. His journey reignites his relationship with his home community, culture, and family.

Podcast
All My Relations, hosted by Matika Wilbur (Swinomish and Tulalip) and Adrienne Keene (Cherokee Nation). <www.allmyrelationspodcast.com/>.
This podcast explores Indigenous perspectives of relationships to each other, land, and our "creatural relatives," addressing topics such as the Land Back movement, Indigenous sovereignty, and kinship systems.

"7 × 7 Generations: Everything we do now will impact our grandchildren for 7 generations. If we discontinue our negligence, we can change things around."

—BIIDASSIGE-BA, JOSEPHINE-BA MANDAMIN,
Ogimaa Water Walker Kwe, Wiikwemkoong Unceded Territory,
Manitoulin Island, Anishinaabe/Odawa Nation, Wawaazisii Dodaim,
Three Fires Lodge Mide Kwe

"We Are the Bundle"
Activating Indigenous Ancestral Powers

DR. TASHA BEEDS is an Indigenous scholar of nêhiyaw, Scottish-Métis, and Bajan ancestry. She activates from connected roles: as a mother, kôhkom, creative artist, poet, Water Walker, and Midewiwin woman from Minweyweywigaan Lodge out of Roseau River First Nations and Wiikwemkoong Unceded Reserve. Her work celebrates Indigeneity, promoting Indigenous nationhood and sovereignty as well as protection of the Land and Waters by carrying Indigenous Ancestral legacies forward for future generations.

———

OUR RESPECTIVE INDIGENOUS spiritual prophecies told us about the arrival of a people who would bring with them a different kind of energy to Turtle Island well before they ever set foot here. Indigenous Ancestors, with their ability to look ahead, saw the immense pain, difficulties, and challenges we, their future generations, would face because of these colonial energies. From the residential school system, to the Sixties Scoop, to today's apprehension of our children, to the racism and violence in all its forms against our women, men, children, the Lands and Waters, and all of Creation, the battles remain the same across the span of time— but so does the love held alive inside our own Indigenous ways of knowing and being in the world.

If you are of clear Indigenous ancestry—meaning you can trace your lines generationally through *numerous Indigenous people*—then you can activate by tapping into the energy of the very Lands and Waters you exist *with*. If you are of clear Indigenous ancestry, your relatives have been here on the place known as Turtle Island since time immemorial, and they love you immensely.

If you are non-Indigenous, your Ancestors are in other Lands. Some non-Indigenous people may have been here as colonial settlers for six or maybe even seven generations, but Indigenous people have been here for thousands of generations. This sheer existence over generations of time gives us a potency non-Indigenous colonizers have been desperate to destroy. We see this attempted destruction in genocidal policies covered in whitewashed paternalistic paper, where our children and women are the primary targets, and our men, gender-fluid relatives, and those who define themselves outside colonial constructs are collaterally aimed at and equally harmed.

The colonial attempt to eradicate us never works, however, because we always remember who we are as Indigenous people. We remember how to activate the generational power intrinsic to the Lands and Waters we continue to have relationships with and, more importantly, *through*. The Lands and Waters are entry points where we can enter other realms that connect us to Creation, as well as to the love of our Ancestors and our future generations. Our conceptualizations of time show us those future generations are here with us now, as are those Old Ones, our Ancestors.

It doesn't matter where you are—city or small town, rez or bush, round dance or kitchen table, lodge or late-night restaurant—every time you pray, you activate; every time you sing, you activate; every time you give offerings or tobacco, you activate; every time you lift Pipes and Water, lift pen to write and fingers to type, sweat and fast, or dance, you activate.

We often think of our spiritual bundles as collections of the articles we have earned: your hand-drum, shaker, Pipe, regalia; but as Josephine-Ba Mandamin, our Anishinaabe mentor, teacher, lead Water Walker, and Nohkomis (Grandmother) Biidaasige-Ba, used to tell us: "You are the bundle." Because you are a sacred bundle, the Land and Waters know when you activate along with the Beings of the Land, Waters, and Sky; literally, all of Creation knows when you activate. Your physical presence is bound by concepts of place, but from an Indigenous perspective, your Spirit is not. Your intent and your heart can move your Spirit to places beyond a non-Indigenous reference. You don't have to be in a specific place to activate. Let your Spirit do the work through the avenues given to each of us by our respective Ancestors. You can do this work by walking outside your door and sitting on the Land or by the Water. Whether you are in a city or on a reserve, if you are on Turtle Island, you are in Indigenous territories and, as a result, you can activate through the means gifted to us by our respective Ancestors. Your power to activate is, of course, stronger in your own traditional Indigenous territories, but you can call on your Ancestors wherever you are and enter into a relationship with the territories of the Indigenous Nations where you are a guest.

This guest status applies to non-Indigenous people in their entirety.[1] Some non-Indigenous people have done, or are beginning to do, the work to understand their responsibilities and obligations as guests on Indigenous territories. Some have not. Those who have sought out understanding and knowledge of their own accord, in a good way, should step up to educate their own people and address negative behaviour. It is not up to Indigenous people to shoulder non-Indigenous work that, by definition, does not belong to us. When we take on non-Indigenous responsibilities, we risk neglecting our own knowledges, intellectual legacies, and spiritual understandings—and our own communities and Nations.

As Indigenous people, we have to focus on ourselves so we can ensure our relatives know how to access the gifts and power left to them. Our Ancestors have left us so many keys to an incredibly powerful knowledge base. It is up to us to start picking them up and walking through the many doorways they left us. You can seek out this knowledge. Ask people. Listen to Elders or read their words. Go to Ceremonies. Sit with the Lands and Waters or walk in Ceremony for them. Let the animals, the medicines, the insects, the trees, let all of Creation teach you. Use social media to learn. Better yet, go visit an Elder, an Aunty, an Uncle, a Grandmother, or a Grandfather. Take them for a drive. Take them to the Water or to the Land. Listen to their stories. They are a part of the bundle. Form no judgment of the Ones who are still battling the colonial energies in the form of drugs or alcohol or are steeped in dysfunction, as their Spirits are connected, too. Every single Indigenous person has access to these gifts and can make a choice to pick them up or not.

---

1   See Dakota Swiftwolfe, *Indigenous Ally Toolkit* (Montreal Urban Aboriginal Community Strategy Network, 2019), www.segalcentre.org/common/sitemedia/201819_Shows/ENG_AllyTookit.pdf; Ruth Koleszar-Green, "What Is a Guest? What Is a Settler?" *Cultural and Pedagogical Inquiry* 10, no. 2 (Fall 2018), journals.library.ualberta.ca/cpi/index.php/cpi/article/view/29452/21463.

We need to continue to activate for Creation more than we ever have before. We need each other and the power of that collectivity as those energies that disregard the life of our future generations continue to try to assert themselves. Our survival is dependent on our own actions; it does not rest within any hands or institutions external to us.

Activate Indigenous languages, governance systems, matriarchies, spiritual teachings, youth and children, education systems, cultural systems, food systems, birthing and transitioning, songs, dances, stories...activate everything the colonizers have tried to destroy, steal, or appropriate. Therein lies the key to our survival and our power. The colonial energy wants this ancestral power, but it simply cannot access it, no matter what.

You are a key, too. We are all collectively the keys—no matter what Indigenous Nation you originate from or where you are physically, you are an Indigenous sacred bundle, and there is power in that collectivity, as our inherent, continual survival shows us.

Keep connecting, and keep drawing and harnessing that power and building it up. Our Ancestors did so for us, just as we are doing for our future generations. "We are the bundle," and it is up to us to carry our Ancestors, ourselves, and our future generations while continuing to remember the rest of Creation. Our survival as humans depends on it.

Educator Connections

Read the editors' thoughts and engage in reflection. Respond to the questions that follow on your own or with your colleague(s).

PERSONAL CONNECTIONS

Christine: Dr. Tasha Beeds's words are soothing to my over-anxious mind. I read her essay as I was reflecting on my obligations to land, water, and other relations, and her words opened the door to finding those answers. As someone who admittedly feels disconnected from the land due to living in an urban centre away from the traditional land-based practices of my ancestors, for me her words evoked a renewed sense of connection or "activation." I appreciate her examples of how we can build our bundles. I also admire the fact that she excels in the realms of both Western academia and traditional Indigenous knowledges, dedicating a lot of her time to learning from Elders. I aspire to attain this balance of knowledge seeking.

Katya: Dr. Tasha Beeds's voice seems to be speaking primarily to Indigenous readers, and I recognize that I cannot activate in the ways she describes. My ancestors are "in other Lands." However, I feel that she is guiding me toward how to help in other forms: by de-activating my own colonial energies and tendencies and taking responsibility in an active way. I think this essay teaches about activism. As both a settler and a guest, I am not a bundle—but how can I support the bundle? I can look for opportunities to help others activate, or simply stay out of the way and learn from people as they pick up their keys and walk through doorways their ancestors have left, as Tasha puts it. This is still work, and requires careful reflection and strength from community.

EDUCATOR INQUIRY AND ACTIONS

- Identify examples of when "colonial energies" take hold of your teaching practices. Discuss strategies for shifting this feeling to be more in line with Indigenous practices.

- Dr. Tasha Beeds provides many starting points for activating one's Indigenous knowledge. If you are Indigenous, choose one and begin or continue your journey. If you are a settler on Indigenous territories, make a list of the ways in which you can "de-activate" your colonial energies and identify individual work that still needs to be done.

- Do you think teaching includes a spiritual element? Explain your thoughts.

- Has this essay shifted your perspective of Indigenous knowledge and the power of ancestral connections within your teaching practices? If so, how?

- What are some ways in which Indigenous ancestral knowledge can be harnessed to empower Indigenous students and promote cultural revitalization?

- How might you bring teachings into your classroom that connect beyond the scope of one generation's knowledge? For example, could you encourage grandparents to become involved?

- In this essay, Dr. Tasha Beeds shares, "We are all collectively the keys—no matter what Indigenous Nation you originate from or where you are physically, you are an Indigenous sacred bundle, and there is power in that collectivity, as our inherent, continual survival shows us." Reflect on how this sentence underscores the importance of collective action and unity in promoting Indigenous knowledge and cultural preservation. Consider this idea in relation to your own teaching.

Classroom Connections

Introduce to students the narrative and the Connected Concepts you wish to focus on. Use the following questions, prompts, and resource suggestions to guide student learning.

CONNECTED CONCEPTS

- Ancestry
- Kinship
- Spiritual bundles

CONNECTING TO SELF: PROMPTS FOR PERSONAL REFLECTION

) Beginning

- Do you ever feel as though you bring a "different energy" than people around you or in specific settings such as school? How so?

- Where are your ancestors from? What kind of ancestor are you going to be? What do you see when you look ahead to seven generations from now?

- What are your treaty responsibilities?

- Where are your lands of origin? Have you been to your homelands?

● **Beyond**

- Of all the systemic and structural ways to activate that Dr. Beeds describes (including Indigenous languages, governance systems, spiritual teachings, youth and children, education systems, cultural systems, food systems, songs, dances, and stories), which one speaks to you and your powerful next steps?

- Do you call upon your ancestors for help when you need it? How do you do this?

CONNECTING TO COMMUNITY: PROMPTS FOR LEARNING CIRCLES

❭ **Beginning**

- Share some of the ways you "activate" or find motivation to take action.

- Practise introducing yourself and where you come from.

❭ **Bridging**

- Dr. Tasha Beeds states, "Our Ancestors have left us so many keys to an incredibly powerful knowledge base." Share some of the keys you have been gifted by your Ancestors.

- Discuss some of the terms Dr. Tasha Beeds has chosen to use and capitalize in her essay, and why you think she decided to do so.

● **Beyond**

- Share your understandings of the differences between stories and prophecies and their significance to your life.

- What types of knowledge, skills, and understandings do you think future generations will need to live more sustainably?

CONNECTING TO LAND-BASED LEARNING

❭ **Beginning**

- Dr. Tasha Beeds provides a long list of starting points for activating one's knowledge and gives inspiration for taking action. Choose one aspect of land or water that you want to learn more about, and begin a journey of your own.

- Read a story about water, then go on a walk and express gratitude for the water you encounter. Learn a water song and sing to the water. Give an offering to the water with the direction of a local Elder or Knowledge Keeper.

❭ **Bridging**

- What places help you activate your knowledges? Reflect on why this is, and then take time to visit one of those places.

- Sit on the land and observe your surroundings. What do you see? What are the land, water, and sky telling you?

● **Beyond**

- Write, revise, and share a land acknowledgement that addresses how you activate your Indigenous gifts or your responsibilities as a guest.

- Map a path of the intersecting ideas connected to land that are discussed in this essay.

CONNECTING TO LAND BACK

- Dr. Tasha Beeds passionately points out a key tension between the power of colonial systems and the power of individual and collective Indigenous identities. This essay reminds readers of the genocidal systems and structures that activated "colonial energies" to systemically disconnect Indigenous Peoples from their lands. These are the systems and histories that the Land Back movement is resurging against. One way Beeds models decolonial activation is through Water Walking. Water Walking is connected to traditional ceremony and roles of women, as well as to contemporary issues surrounding safe water (and saving water) and health.[2] Activism can take many forms. How is Water Walking unique to the Land Back movement?

CONNECTIONS TO OTHER INDIGENOUS RESOURCES

Books

Be a Good Ancestor, by Leona Prince and Gabrielle Prince (Orca Book Publishers, 2022; ages 3–5).
This beautifully illustrated picture book emphasizes the many ways we can learn to be good ancestors to land, water, and living things through our ideas and feelings.

Visions of the Crow (Dreams, Vol. 1), by Wanda John-Kehewin (HighWater Press, 2023; ages 12–18).
In this graphic novel, high school senior Damon embarks on a spiritual journey through time and space that highlights the healing power of understanding one's history.

Last Standing Woman, by Winona LaDuke (HighWater Press, 2023).
This adult novel chronicles the struggles and resilience of the White Earth Anishinaabe people from the 1800s to the early 2000s as they face the devastating impacts of European colonization.

Film

The Water Walker, directed by James Burns (Seeing Red, 2020). <www.seeingred6nations.com/film>.
This award-winning short documentary is about the activism of Anishinaabekwe Autumn Peltier, Indigenous global leader and activist, alongside artwork by Christi Belcourt. It addresses water and land injustices in Canada and beyond.

---

2   CBC News, "Water Walkers: Indigenous Women Draw on Tradition to Raise Environmental Awareness," September 4, 2015, www.cbc.ca/radio/unreserved/unreserved-radio-indigenous-on-cbc-radio-one-sept-6-1.3215919/water-walkers-indigenous-women-draw-on-tradition-to-raise-environmental-awareness-1.3216495; Mother Earth Water Walk, "About Us," www.motherearthwaterwalk.com/?page_id=11.

Online

Indigenous Ally Toolkit, by Dakota Swiftwolfe (Montreal Urban Aboriginal Community Strategy Network, 2019). <www.segalcentre.org/common /sitemedia/201819_Shows/ENG_AllyTookit.pdf>.
This document supports learning how to be an ally, accomplice, or co-resistor to Indigenous people, providing helpful questions and a step-by-step guide for settlers.

Mother Earth Water Walk. <www.motherearthwaterwalk.com/#gallery-1>.
This website provides resources centred on water, including documentation of Water Walks, songs, videos, photos, and water news and events.

Their Voices Will Guide Us: Student and Youth Engagement Guide, by Charlene Bearhead (National Inquiry into Missing and Murdered Indigenous Women and Girls, 2018). <www.mmiwg-ffada.ca/wp-content/uploads/2018/11 /NIMMIWG-THEIR-VOICES-WILL-GUIDE-US.pdf>
A comprehensive resource with guidance for all ages to begin conversations around gender roles, anti-racism, colonial violence, and empowering people to find their voices to respond and take action.

Podcast

"Tasha Beeds: Walking With Water," *What About Water? with Jay Famiglietti*," Season 3, Episode 9.February 16, 2022. <podcasts.apple.com/ca/podcast /tasha-beeds-walking-with-water/id1485919205?i=1000551240271>.
Dr. Tasha Beeds discusses the origins of Water Walking as Indigenous ceremony.

Land Back and *Dance as Though the Ancestors Are Watching*

SONNY ASSU, Ligwiłda'xw of the Kwakwa̱ka'wakw Nations, is an interdisciplinary artist whose work focuses on pop culture, nostalgia, colonialism, and Indigenous futurism. His award-winning art uses autobiographical, humorous, and political elements to explore the realities of being Indigenous in the colonial state of Canada. Sonny holds both bachelor's and master's degrees in fine arts (Emily Carr University, Concordia University). His work is included in numerous major public collections, including the National Gallery of Canada (Ottawa) and the Museum of Anthropology (Vancouver).

VISUAL PROPAGANDA has always interested me, because it melds language and aesthetics to present a finite way of how we should be thinking.

Propaganda is a manipulative form of the dissemination of information—whether it be factual or false—to influence public opinion. Visual propaganda uses symbols, words, and gestures in an aesthetic way to change the way we think, feel, or act. It was most notably used in the early to mid-20th century during the First and Second World Wars by both the "allies" and the "enemy."[1] Propaganda often carries negative connotations,

---

1   For more information on propaganda, particularly during the Second World War, see Facing History & Ourselves, "The Impact of Nazi Propaganda: Visual Essay," www.facinghistory.org/resource-library/visual-essay-impact-propaganda.

but it has been used to spread positive messages as well. Modern propaganda is omnipresent in social media, advertising, and consumerism.

In 2019, Land and Water defenders erected blockades and checkpoints in Wet'suwet'en territory (in what is now referred to as northern British Columbia). Their aim was to protect the land from a natural-gas pipeline being constructed through the unceded territory without the consent of the hereditary leadership of the Wet'suwet'en people. I made these images in response to the colonial state of Canada sending militarized RCMP officers to confront Land and Water defenders, in order to demonstrate my support for them.

Protests in solidarity sprang up across the country, with the meme-worthy chants of "Land Back!" demanding that governments hold themselves responsible and accountable for their actions. During this time, I witnessed Indigenous youth stand up to the oppression, segregation, and systemic racism that Canada was built on. I feel pride in how they conducted and carried themselves, respecting each other and the land they stood upon. They move through this world with their kin behind them: *they dance as though the ancestors are watching.*

Educator Connections

Read the editors' thoughts and engage in reflection. Respond to the questions that follow on your own or with your colleague(s).

PERSONAL CONNECTIONS

Christine: I admire how, as Indigenous people, we use our gifts and talents to advocate for each other. Seeing how Sonny Assu uses his artistic talent to advocate for "land back" prompts me to ask myself how I can use my voice as an educator to advocate for the same. I was keeping an eye on the news and social media surrounding the protests on Wet'suwet'en territory, and my heart felt the weight of hundreds of years of so-called progress when the Canadian state responded with the might of militarized force rather than understanding and dialogue. I appreciate how,

Land Back, 2020
Digital Image
24.5 × 36.5 in / 62.25 × 91.45 cm
(Image courtesy of the artist
and the Equinox Gallery.)

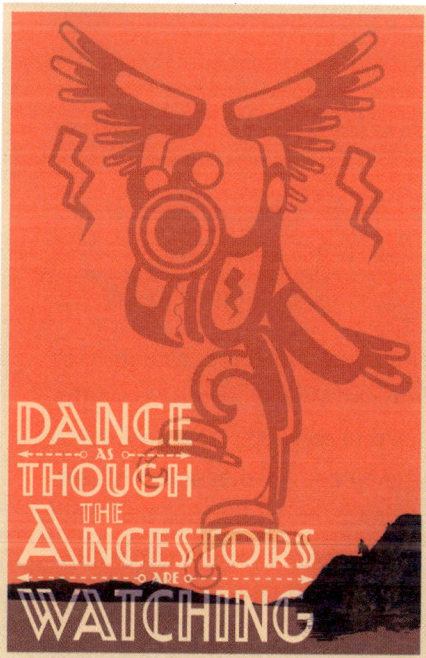

*Dance as Though the Ancestors Are
Watching, 2020*
Digital Image
24.5 × 36.5 in / 62.25 × 91.45 cm
(Image courtesy of the artist
and the Equinox Gallery.)

through art and visual propaganda, Sonny casts a spotlight on the defiance, strength, and resilience of the Wet'suwet'en land defenders.

Katya: I find Sonny Assu's work so creative in its forms and functions. In my undergraduate courses, I remember encountering the idea of "socialist realism" and how dictatorships tried to control the public through imagery that conveyed a message beneficial to their particular aims. This was before the context of social media and sophisticated visual marketing, but nonetheless, images were cleverly used to appeal to multiple age groups. The role of images and digital texts continues to become increasingly sophisticated and serves many functions; however, some of the visual manipulation strategies remain eerily similar—reminding me of the importance of being critical of information that comes through images and teaching youth how such messages work on them. When I think about news stories about Missing and Murdered Indigenous Women and Girls being found in landfills or the war on Ukrainian soil, it is evident that visual propaganda is still being used in dangerous and divisive ways. Assu reminds readers about its potential to reveal socio-political commentary and influence us in positive and transformative ways as well.

EDUCATOR INQUIRY AND ACTIONS

- Sonny Assu describes how Indigenous youth took action against systemic racism in Canada. As a school team, identify and examine positive examples of youth demonstrating activism and taking anti-oppressive stances.

- Walk through the halls of your school, paying particular attention to the messages students receive in this space. Whose writing is on the walls? What images are present? Who is represented? How do images and printed text work together, and do they convey messages that are positive and affirming to the community? As an individual teacher, think about these ideas in the context of your classroom.

- Work with your students to decide on a social issue that is relevant to them. Invite students to work in groups to think of a message they want to convey in relation to the issue and determine how they can do so using few words and one image. This is a great community-building exercise, as the student work can be shared and displayed for the whole school.

- What different actions might you take if you knew Elders and Ancestors were watching?

- Create a response to a current human-rights issue (e.g., racism, gender phobia, discriminatory policies) that melds language and aesthetics.

Classroom Connections

Introduce to students the artwork and narrative and the Connected Concepts you wish to focus on. Use the following questions, prompts, and resource suggestions to guide student learning.

CONNECTED CONCEPTS
- Consumerism
- Advertising
- Critical literacy
- Indigenous aesthetics

CONNECTING TO SELF: PROMPTS FOR PERSONAL REFLECTION
) Beginning
- What do you see in the images? What is being represented?

- How do these images make you feel? For example, do you feel guilt, hope, anger, or pride, or perhaps you feel mixed emotions?

) Bridging
- Why do you think Sonny Assu chose the colours he used in these pieces?

- How do your own biases influence how you interpret these images?

- How are you influenced by social media and consumerism?

- **Beyond**
  - How does Assu's art "change the way we think, feel, or act"?

  - What are some differences between positive images or messages and those used to spread negative perspectives?

CONNECTING TO COMMUNITY: PROMPTS FOR LEARNING CIRCLES

- **Beginning**
  - Discuss the terms *trope*, *cliché*, and *meme* and your understandings of their influence on societal values or beliefs.

- **Bridging**
  - Discuss the message of each of Sonny Assu's works featured here. Think about the overall message communicated to you as a viewer when you consider them together.

  - Consider and discuss how modern technologies are influencing Indigenous traditions or practices.

- **Beyond**
  - Share some ways images are used today to influence, teach, subvert, or inspire.

  - Share a social issue you think deserves more attention. What medium would be a good fit to communicate a message about this issue to a specific audience?

  - Share your opinions on both the overt and silent ways social media and consumerism affect your relationships with people and with land and water.

CONNECTING TO LAND-BASED LEARNING

- **Beginning**
  - Locate Wet'suwet'en territory or the territory of Kwakwa̱ka'wakw Nation, Sonny Assu's community, on a map. What can you find out about the community, including the agreements made on the land?

> **Bridging**

- Look at advertisements that promote and are connected to outdoor experiences, such as those for a store that sells camping gear. How does the advertisement work to convince you that you need to buy certain items to have an experience or survive on the land?

- Try to disconnect from social media, online advertising and shopping, and other forms of visual manipulation and consumerism for a sustained period. Connect to land instead. What did you notice within yourself? Was it a challenge to do this?

● **Beyond**

- Create a textual juxtaposition to convey a message that reveals a societal flaw, problem, or issue. You could do this by creating a sketch or digital image of a place or by taking a photo on the land and juxtaposing it with a slogan from popular culture, a trope, or a cliché.

- Look at news articles about land claims or Indigenous land disputes and consider the images presented with these stories. Can you translate these images in your own drawing or image to synthesize the overall message?

CONNECTING TO LAND BACK

- There is a tension between traditional and contemporary representations in Sonny Assu's artwork. Spend time analyzing the visual elements of the piece *Land Back*. Then, pair his art with imagery in a news story or social media post that connects to the Land Back movement. What types of symbols, colours, lines, shapes, or cultural representations are present?

- Sonny Assu once shared that he used a '90s rock poster aesthetic "to convey the message about the importance of returning control of our lands, waters, and natural resources back to the hands of the original caretakers" (Sonny Assu, 2023, personal communication). Research other Indigenous artists who convey strong Land Back messages and consider the different aesthetics or artistic choices (e.g., mediums, styles) used to represent their messages. How do these artistic elements work to convey the message of Land Back?

115

CONNECTIONS TO OTHER INDIGENOUS RESOURCES

Books

The Elders Are Watching, by David Bouchard (Raincoast Books, 2003; ages 9 and up).
Featuring rhythmic text and the striking artwork of Roy Henry Vickers, this picture book delivers an important message about protecting the Earth for future generations.

Beau Dick: Devoured by Consumerism, by LaTiesha Fazakas, John Cussans, and Candice Hopkins (Figure 1 Publishing, 2019).
This book shares images from the final art exhibit of Kwakw<u>aka</u>'wakw Northwest Coast Chief and artist Beau Dick.

Perception, by KC Adams (HighWater Press, 2019).
This text features striking photographs of individuals accompanied by stereotyped perceptions about them juxtaposed with their real identities. A free teacher guide is available.

Sonny Assu: A Selective History, by Sonny Assu, with Candice Hopkins, Marianne Nicolson, Richard Van Camp, and Ellyn Walker (Heritage House, 2018).
This book features Sonny Assu's artwork alongside essays that describe the significance of the aesthetic activism of his art and its connections to broader Indigenous movements.

Online

Idle No More. <idlenomore.ca>.
This site shares the history of the Idle No More movement, as well as current campaigns and activism. It also provides resources for further education.

Sonny Assu | Interdisciplinary Artist. <www.sonnyassu.com>.
This site provides images of many of Assu's works, as well as artist statements to inspire new ways of engaging with his art.

Podcast

"Creative Resistance," *Landback for the People*, Season 1, Episode 5, hosted by Nick Tilsen. <www.youtube.com/watch?v=VM0xReVN-P4>.
This podcast provides an American perspective of the Indigenous Land Back movement. This episode focuses on the intersection of activism and artists.

Qamani'tuaq
(ᖃᒪᓂᑦᐊᖅ) Perspectives

The grade 6 students who took the photographs featured in this section attend Jonah Amitnaaq Secondary School in Baker Lake, a community located in Nunavut's Kivalliq Region. They are: Inuksaq Angotingoar, Makayla Aupaluktuq, Brendan Kingilik, Carina Kingilik, Kyle Lareau, Quin Mikkungwak, Selena Narkyagik, Kaylee Rumbolt, Marissa Scottie, Nathan Snow, Connor Tagoona-Niego, Koen Tapatai, and Shelly Tunguaq. The community's Inuktitut name is Qamani'tuaq (ᖃᒪᓂᑦᐊᖅ), which means "where the river widens." This refers to the community's position next to Baker Lake, which is fed by the Thelon and Kazan Rivers. All of the students were raised in Baker Lake and most of the students are Inuit.

THE STUDENTS completed this project with the guidance of their teacher, Colleen Chau, as part of a social studies unit focused on current-day Nunavut. Students took these photos in the course of their everyday lives and during the school's two annual land trips. The fall trip takes place before the snow arrives, and the spring trip takes place when the lake is frozen. Each trip takes place at a location several kilometres outside of Baker Lake. The trips give students an opportunity to get out on the land and live and practise their Inuit cultural tradition with local Knowledge Keepers through activities such as berry picking, fishing, jigging (ice fishing), and making bannock and caribou stew. On the land, students learn and demonstrate knowledge, expertise, thoughtfulness, and camaraderie that cannot be seen in the traditional classroom.

The images offer a view of the land and water in and around Baker Lake through the eyes of the 11- and 12-year-old students, and the places and experiences that are unique to them.

Top left: This is a walrus getting hunted in Igloolik on the Arctic Ocean. It is cool that they are hunting a walrus. I have hunted a caribou (tuktu), but I've never hunted a walrus.
— INUKSAQ ANGOTINGOAR

Top right: This is a seal that a couple of adults and teenagers hunted on the Arctic Ocean. They wanted to give the seal to the Elders. I felt disgusted because the look of the blood was making me nauseous.
— MAKAYLA AUPALUKTUQ

Bottom: This is me drawing with my feet when I was really bored on the ice fishing trip in Baker Lake. I had a bit of fun at the end when we were sliding on the ice.
— CONNOR TAGOONA-NIEGO

Top left: I took this picture of the sunset when I was with my cousin and her family at the cabin because it looked so beautiful. I felt so happy I was at the land. We don't go to the land that much, but when we do, we mostly play around or go fishing.
—QUIN MIKKUNGWAK

Top right: This is the summer sun setting behind the snow fence in Baker Lake.
—CARINA KINGILIK

Bottom: This is a sunset in Baker Lake. This is looking at the Igloo Hotel and the Airport Road. It reminds me of my uncle and driving around in Baker Lake, and it feels fun.
—KAYLEE RUMBOLT

Top: This is the snow fence that was built in Baker Lake in 2010 to stop the snow from coming into town and burying houses. It is fun driving on the airport road and seeing the clean and wonderful land, and calming to hear the soft wind against the window.
—NATHAN SNOW

Right: This is a fishing hole in the ice of Baker Lake. It was fun making this hole, but it was really hard to make. I was fishing for a long time, but I didn't catch a fish.
—SELENA NARKYAGIK

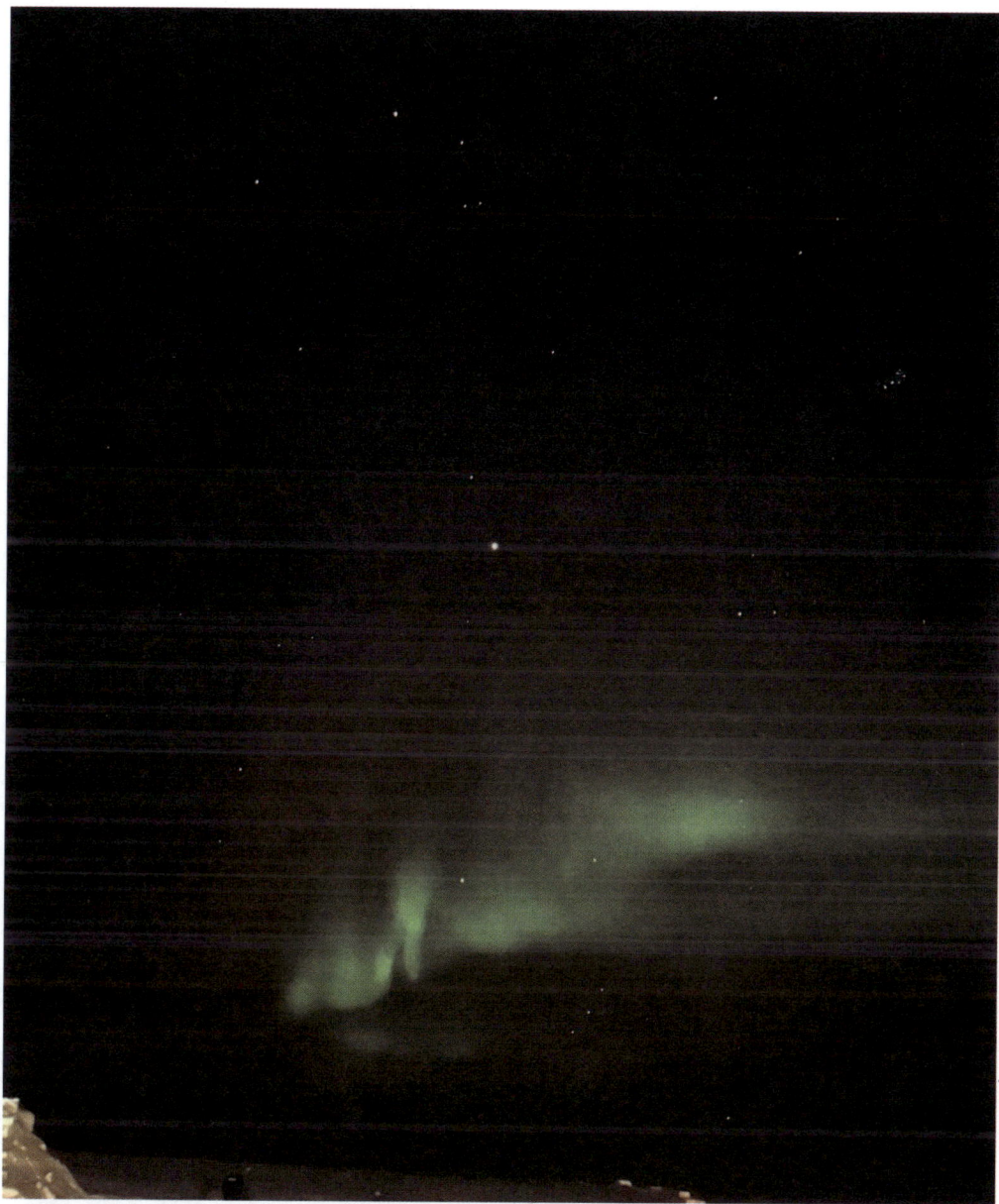

I like the northern lights and how they are the colour green. The Inuit have a superstition that when we play with our zippers outside, the northern lights are going to kill or kidnap us. When we whistle, the northern lights will dance around.

—MARISSA SCOTTIE

Opposite top: This is our class leaving the campsite at Hagliq Island. It shows the tents and skidoos pulling the sleds (qamutiks) away.
—BRENDAN KINGILIK

Opposite bottom: I took this picture from inside the sled (qamutik) of the other skidoos pulling the other sleds (qamutik) with students in them. We are heading back to Baker Lake from Hagliq Island.
—SHELLY TUNGUAQ

Top: This is a picture of either a sunrise or sunset. I don't remember which, because I took this picture a couple years ago. The picture looks cool and calming. I really like the vibes this picture gives.
—KYLE LAREAU

Bottom: This is a picture of a fishing place. The fish bite right away here, and the water is open all year round.
—KOEN TAPATAI

Educator Connections

Read the editors' thoughts and engage in reflection. Respond to the questions that follow on your own or with your colleague(s).

PERSONAL CONNECTIONS

Christine: What a beautiful collaborative photo essay! The students were given an open-ended prompt to take pictures of meaningful places centred on land and water—and this is what they came up with. I love seeing the images they selected to share! The photographs of the landscapes showing sunsets seemingly touching the Earth in the distance are my favourites. Visiting the North is a bucket-list experience for me, and these images make me want to experience the vast landscape even more. This year, my students began an exchange program, and a group of 10 students from Naujaat, Nunavut, visited us in Winnipeg. It was most of the students' first time in the city, and it was an incredible experience to see it through their eyes. I'm excited to have the experience of visiting them too.

Katya: Several years ago, an Inuk marine biologist spoke in a class I was taking on Indigenous methodologies. Hearing about her inspiring research helped me think about the diverse traditions that exist within Arctic regions. I do not know very much about Nunavut, the Northwest Territories, and the Yukon. My knowledge comes from my mom's stories of travelling to remote northern communities or from information shared by teachers who may not have even travelled there. I think many teachers plan lessons about places we have never been. The students' photographs show how land-based experiences offer an opportunity to not only learn about but also practise cultural traditions. For educators, coordinating experiences like this is a team effort, and I can see how a great deal of learning can come from just the planning. These photos provide a breath of fresh air, opening a window into what is possible for both teachers and students.

- Organize a land-based photography project with your class, grade group, or school community. This could become part of a collective social studies project tied to a bigger inquiry question or idea.

- What types of relationships are needed for an exchange between students in an Indigenous community and those in a non-Indigenous community? It is important to ensure partnerships are meaningful and not one-off engagements. How could your school team make connections to an Indigenous community and begin building land-based inquiries in a reciprocal way (such as sharing about land in both places and engaging with Indigenous approaches that can help make new meaning of your environment)? Refer to the "getting started" steps on page 15.

- How do these photographs represent learning? Think about them in relation to the most recent photos you took in your classroom learning environment. What does the comparison of these two sets of photos reveal about your teaching practices and your goals and vision?

- How is the Arctic or the North constructed in current provincial or territorial curriculum documents? What perspective is missing from these documents, and how can the student photos featured here be a catalyst for this learning?

- Organize a land trip. List all the things you need to do in preparation. Submit a proposal for funding to make it happen.

- How do you provide spaces, places, and opportunities for students to live and practise their cultural traditions?

Classroom Connections

Introduce to students the photographs and captions and the Connected Concepts you wish to focus on. Use the following questions, prompts, and resource suggestions to guide student learning.

CONNECTED CONCEPTS

- Inuit Qaujimajatuqangit (IQ)[1]
- Hunting and fishing sustainably
- Perspective
- Digital photography

CONNECTING TO SELF: PROMPTS FOR PERSONAL REFLECTION

❯ Beginning

- What do you know or want to know about the Arctic?

- What did you learn about everyday life in Nunavut from looking at these photos?

❯ Bridging

- What do you notice about the interplay between these youth and their environment? What aspects of their relationship with the land resonate with your own connection to nature?

- What points of view (e.g., close-up, bird's-eye view) are represented in the photos? How does this perspective affect your focus, attention, or connection as a viewer?

---

1   Inuit Qaujimajatuqangit (IQ) is the term used to describe "Inuit epistemology or the Indigenous knowledge of the Inuit"; it translates as "that which Inuit have always known to be true." For more information, see Shirley Tagalik, "Inuit Qaujimajatuqangit: The Role of Indigenous Knowledge in Supporting Wellness in Inuit Communities in Nunavut," Child and Youth Health: Inuit Fact Sheet (National Collaborating Centre for Aboriginal Health, 2009–10), www.ccnsa-nccah.ca/docs/fact%20sheets/child%20and%20youth/Inuit%20IQ%20EN%20web.pdf.

- Reflect on the images that depict traditional activities like hunting or fishing. How do these activities demonstrate a sustainable way of life that is deeply rooted in the environment? What can we learn from these practices?

- What do you know about the Arctic and where has this knowledge come from? What stereotypes have you been taught about the Arctic? What do you need to unlearn?

- Choose one image from the essay that illustrates the importance of collective responsibility and Indigenous wisdom in ensuring a healthy ecosystem. How does this image portray that?

CONNECTING TO COMMUNITY: PROMPTS FOR LEARNING CIRCLES

❭ Beginning

- Share the image that stood out to you the most and explain why.

- Share a natural landform that you notice in your community.

❭ Bridging

- Share what you wonder about Nunavut.

- These photos are windows into experiences unique to 11- and 12-year-old students. What photos do you have in your photo library of unique places or experiences? Share the story of one place or experience and why it is important and unique to you.

● Beyond

- Discuss how these images represent resiliency, ingenuity, and land-based knowledges.

- Reflect on the challenges of a land-based excursion such as those shown in some of the photos and how they might be overcome. Think from the perspective of the students and their families, the teachers, and the community.

CONNECTING TO LAND-BASED LEARNING

❯ Beginning

- Locate Baker Lake, a community located in Nunavut's Kivalliq Region, on a map. What can you find out about the community, including the agreements made on the land?

- View photographs of Nunavut from social media, such as those at Destination Nunavut <destinationnunavut.ca/destinations/kivalliq-region /baker-lake>. Compare and contrast the imagery, language, subjects, and perspectives portrayed in the photos and captions.

- With your classmates, create a photo essay of your community. Hold a gallery walk and reflect on what you notice about the images chosen.

❯ Bridging

- What are the Indigenous place names in your area? How do they connect to the land?

- Learn about and play an Inuit traditional game.[2] What values might this game instill in those who play?

● Beyond

- Look at photos from your experiences on the land. Think about the types of perspectives represented in the photos (e.g., close-ups, landscapes). Write a caption for one or more photos for a variety of audiences and purposes; for example, a caption that inspires or teaches.

- During their land trips, the students were living and practising their Inuit cultural traditions alongside local Knowledge Keepers. Where would you go to have the opportunity to practise land-based knowledges or your own cultural traditions?

---

2   For more information, see Traditional Inuit Games <www.athropolis.com/news-upload/master/11-frames .htm>, a website created by students in Iqaluit, Nunavut. The Arctic Winter Games <arcticwintergames .net/About-AWG>, which celebrate the sport and cultural heritage of the Arctic, include traditional sports.

CONNECTING TO LAND BACK

- Think about the land-based practices shared by the students, including fishing, jigging (ice fishing), and hunting for walrus and caribou. In the Baker Lake area, resource exploration and mining have interfered and caused disconnections with Inuit rights and cultural practices. The documentary *Inuit Knowledge and Climate Change* and the book *I Will Live for Both of Us: A History of Colonialism, Uranium Mining, and Inuit Resistance* share how Inuit have been affected by environmentally damaging practices and how they are fighting to protect the land and keep alive practices that help sustain the land.[3] Think critically about how colonialism has caused, and continues to cause, disconnections with Inuit rights to land, game management, and cultural practices. How has colonization affected your family's life? Your life?

- In the 1950s, many Inuit families were forcibly relocated farther north by the Canadian government. The government now admits that "Inuit were separated from home communities and extended family[,] were not provided with adequate shelter or supplies, and were not properly informed of where they would be located or for how long."[4] In 2010, the government apologized for the relocations, which would not have happened if Inuit had been allowed to maintain control of their land. In January 2024, Prime Minister Justin Trudeau signed an agreement to transfer control of two million square kilometres of resource-rich Arctic lands to the government of Nunavut.[5] Research more about this historic agreement (the largest land transfer in Canada's history) and think about its significance. How could the transfer of Arctic lands to the government of Nunavut impact the social, economic, and cultural autonomy of Inuit communities?

---

3 *Inuit Knowledge and Climate Change*, Isuma TV, Igloolik Isuma Productions and Kunuk Cohn Productions, 2010, www.isuma.tv/inuit-knowledge-and-climate-change/movie; Joan Scottie, Warren Bernauer, and Jack Hicks, *I Will Live for Both of Us: A History of Colonialism, Uranium Mining, and Inuit Resistance* (University of Manitoba Press, 2022).

4 Government of Canada, "Government of Canada's Apology for the Inuit High Arctic Relocation," www.rcaanc-cirnac.gc.ca/eng/1100100014187/1534785248701.

5 Emma Tranter, "'It's High Time': Nunavut Officially Takes Over Land, Resource Responsibilities From Feds," CBC News, January 18, 2024, www.cbc.ca/news/canada/north/nunavut-trudeau-sign-devolution-argreement-1.7086272.

CONNECTIONS TO OTHER INDIGENOUS RESOURCES

Books

Alego, by Ningeokuluk Teevee (Groundwood Books, 2009; ages 3–7).
From a child's perspective, this picture book shares the story of an Inuit girl who collects clams at the shore with her grandmother. Available in dual-language Inuktitut and English, with a free teacher guide also available.

A Promise Is a Promise, by Michael Kusugak with Robert Munsch (Annick Press, 1988; ages 4–7).
This story features an Inuk girl who learns the importance of listening and staying away from dangers on the ice from an encounter with Qallupilluit, troll-like underwater creatures.

The Right to Be Cold: One Woman's Story of Protecting Her Culture, the Arctic, and the Whole Planet, by Sheila Watt-Cloutier (Allen Lane, 2015).
This non-fiction book for older readers describes award-winning activist Watt-Cloutier's work to preserve the rights of Inuit in the Arctic.

Films

Angry Inuk, directed by Alethea Arnaquq-Baril (National Film Board, 2016). <www.nfb.ca/film/angry_inuk/>.
Award-winning documentary about Inuit using new technology, including social media, to challenge negative perceptions of seal hunting and present themselves to the world as a modern people in dire need of a sustainable economy.

Inuit Knowledge and Climate Change, directed by Zacharias Kunuk and Dr. Ian Mauro (Isuma TV, Igloolik Isuma Productions and Kunuk Cohn Productions, 2010). <www.isuma.tv/inuit-knowledge-and-climate-change/movie>.
This documentary features Inuit perspectives and observations on climate change. Traditional Inuit law, teachings, and land-based knowledges are shared, which document changes to the environment.

Nowhere Land (Inuktitut Version), directed by Rosie Bonnie Ammaaq (National Film Board, 2015). <www.nfb.ca/film/nowhere_land_inuktitut/>.
This documentary provides information about seal hunting and works to counter misperceptions. Study guides are available on the NFB website.

Online

"Celebrating Indigenous History Month," Science World, June 8, 2021.
<www.scienceworld.ca/stories/celebrating-indigenous-history-month/>.
Shares the contributions of Indigenous individuals making an impact in
STEAM (science, technology, engineering, art and design, and math),
including Inuk marine biologist Enooyaq Sudlovenick.

Arctic Council. <arctic-council.org/about/>.
The Arctic Council is an intergovernmental forum consisting of Arctic
states and Indigenous organizations, aimed at promoting co-operation and
addressing common challenges in the Arctic region. Its mission primarily
focuses on environmental protection, sustainable development, and the
well-being of Arctic communities.

Inuit Circumpolar Council. <www.inuitcircumpolar.com/icc-kids/>.
The kids' section of this website includes information, maps, fun facts,
games and apps, and a guide to learning Inuktut.

Inuuqatigiit: Inuit Cultural Online Resource.
.
This website supports student and teacher professional learning. It includes
a series of video podcasts (on topics such as Indigenous knowledge, games,
building, throat singing, traditional knowledge, and a podcast project for
language learning of Inuktitut), teaching resources, and a photo gallery.

"Qamani'tuaq (Baker Lake)_Lars Qaqqaq_Français," Inuit Tapiriit Kanatami.
<www.youtube.com/watch?v=CCNyyo9Rrb8>.
Lars Qaqqaq, from Baker Lake, shares how photography got him into
trapping and helped him develop a love of the land-based lifestyle and an
appreciation of the importance of culture and belonging. Lars is the guide
who accompanied the Jonah Amitnaaq Secondary School on their spring
land trip, which is documented in many of the photos shared here.

PART THREE

DOING

THIS SECTION DIVES into *doing* or taking action. We learn from contributors who have each been inspired by the land and water to take action in creative forms: in physical and digital spaces, through repetition and rhythm, in photographs, and by creating new social networks—both online and on land. They show us how sovereignty and strength can be expressed in many ways, and always with passion and purpose. Learn from shalan joudry (L'nu [Mi'kmaq]), Tricia Logan (Métis), Dakota Bear (Cree), and Shirli Ewanchuk (Ojibway) as they use their voices to share the significance of land and water in their lives and work.

While colonial effects on land have been traumatic and Land Back efforts and resistance are full of layered challenges, the contributors remind us that taking a political stance on land and water can be aesthetically beautiful, appealing, and accessible to a wide range of audiences. Educators dedicated to land-based education face ongoing challenges and unanticipated constraints that test our commitment to action. The contributors in this section share perspectives that encourage us to think poetically, pictorially, and politically to solve problems. As hip-hop artist Dakota Bear states, "as soon as you look for the answer you see the solution" (page 158).

shalan joudry takes readers into the forests of her traditional territories. In her poem "Raising Forests," we are invited to hear the stories of the forest and to stand in solidarity with the trees. joudry brings awareness to the idea that the significance and consequences of one's actions may not be seen in the present moment. She suggests a need for taking sustained action and having the foresight to think generationally.

Scholar Tricia Logan reflects on how her online language-learning experiences connect to specific land-based knowledges, offering a glimpse into her creativity and humility. She shares how the distance necessitated by the

COVID-19 pandemic created challenges for language learners, and how the digital solutions to these challenges revitalized language learning communities, bridging places, landscapes, and knowledge systems all at once.

In his lyrics, Dakota Bear shares the empowering sounds of freedom and advocacy: "Together we started a movement / Together we stand / We shakin' the earth as we move" (page 158). With his powerful phrasing, he draws on the ancestral strength of healers and chiefs. Bear connects to land throughout his song "Freedom," but ultimately focuses on the empowering feeling of freedom and strength that comes from being yourself.

Finally, educator Shirli Ewanchuk describes the process of creating a land-based learning program from the ground up, inspiring us with her vision and accomplishment. When there was no curriculum to guide her, she took action to identify existing underutilized resources she could use to create and revitalize important programming for her community.

This section prompts us to think about doing. What actions have others taken and what actions can we take to raise, revitalize, advocate, envision, create, and stand together? What seeds might you plant? What digital connections can you cultivate? How can you use your voice as a tool for freedom? How might you collaborate with others to create sustainable land-based practices?

CONNECTING ONLINE

Post reflections from your own learning or share how you take up these ideas in your educational setting using the hashtags #FootbridgeRenewalBook and #FootbridgeRenewal.

"Raising Forests"

SHALAN JOUDRY is a L'nu (Mi'kmaw) mother, poet, and ecologist, as well as a playwright, podcaster, oral storyteller, actor, and cultural interpreter.[1] She has published two books of poetry: *Generations Re-merging* (2014) and *Waking Ground* (2020). She lives with her family in their community of L'sətkuk (Bear River First Nation, Nova Scotia), where she is focusing on reclaiming her Mi'kmaw/L'nu language.

---

1   On her website www.shalanjoudry.com, shalan joudry notes: "My personal choice not to capitalize my name (unless beginning a sentence) is to be consistent with how I feel that we are taught as Indigenous peoples to not over-emphasize the self in relation to the collective. I am aware that this [is] not a popular grammar practice in English in Canada, yet it's a stance i have taken at this time."

Raising Forests[2]

we are not the first generation to lose forests
as trees were slain for ships and forts
l'nu hunters were refused entry to their territory
fracturing livelihoods and continuity

in this landscape there have been many ends of the world
as one knows it
parents mourned children at the edges of cliffs
guardians became chained to bottles

to know the stories
as story carriers do
is to constantly taste scars where the wounds
had long punctured through

people already devastated by massacres of forests
each new generation's lost battle to save trees
too many centuries of someone's world in pieces

let's tend to the forests like prophets
encourage them to wilder in old growth
and watch them mature into being

2   "Raising Forests" from *Waking Ground* © 2020 by shalan joudry. Used with permission of Gaspereau Press.

Educator Connections

Read the editors' thoughts and engage in reflection. Respond to the questions that follow on your own or with your colleague(s).

PERSONAL CONNECTIONS

Christine: To me, shalan joudry's poem encapsulates the intergenerational effects of colonialism and disconnection from the land around us. It highlights the connection between our well-being and the well-being of the environment we live in. Strangely, I find myself comforted by the line "in this landscape there have been many ends of the world." Given the current state of the world, it's easy to feel hopeless, but this line reminds me that life goes on and continues despite the tragedies that unfold around us. The line "let's tend to the forest like prophets" is a call to action to protect the natural world even when it might be unpopular to do so.

Katya: When I read shalan joudry's poem out loud, it gives me goosebumps. The idea of raising forests like prophets stands out. I have an eerie feeling when I think of the "massacres of forests," reminding me of all the things around me made from trees; the trauma of trees can be seen in my bookshelves, on the walls, within the walls, everywhere. I can get nervous in the woods, but this poem makes me wonder if the forests are fearful of humans? This poem also reminds me of some lessons, good and bad, that my dad taught me. He taught me to respect the forest and all her inhabitants. The title "Raising Forests" stirs up a renewed sense of the responsibility of raising children—raising children to care about forests, to see trees as more than commodities, so they can "know the stories" rather than "taste scars" and wounds of past actions.

EDUCATOR INQUIRY AND ACTIONS

- What do you think the poem's portrayal of historical loss and resilience in the face of environmental destruction suggests about the enduring strength of Indigenous communities and their relationship with the land?

- Has this poem shifted your perspective on the impacts of deforestation and land dispossession on Indigenous communities and their cultural continuity? If so, how?

- How can we as educators incorporate Indigenous ecological knowledge and perspectives on environmental stewardship into our curriculum and teaching practices?

- Discuss some obstacles to bringing Indigenous knowledge and cultural narratives into the classroom, and brainstorm strategies to overcome these challenges.

- shalan joudry writes, "let's tend to the forests like prophets." Reflect on this line of the poem in relation to your own teaching. How can you inspire your students to develop a deeper connection with the environment and a sense of responsibility for its well-being?

- As a school team, how can you collaborate with local Indigenous communities and organizations to support initiatives focused on environmental stewardship, cultural preservation, and regenerating natural habitats?

Classroom Connections

Introduce to students the poem and the Connected Concepts you wish to focus on. Use the following questions, prompts, and resource suggestions to guide student learning.

CONNECTED CONCEPTS
- Intergenerational trauma
- Environmental protection/stewardship
- Environmental degradation

CONNECTING TO SELF: PROMPTS FOR PERSONAL REFLECTION

❯ Beginning

- What elements of nature do you want to guard and protect?

- What actions can you take to use less paper, or to use products that come from trees in a more sustainable way?

- What trees do you connect to?

❯ Bridging

- What are some obstacles to conserving forests and protecting the environment? How can we overcome these challenges?

- What does it mean to be a prophet?

- What knowledge or stories might trees keep or carry?

● Beyond

- What are some stories of the past you have heard from your family? How do these stories help connect you to your ancestors?

- What lessons can be drawn from this poem to inspire environmental activism and advocacy, particularly in the context of Indigenous land rights and conservation?

- What are some ways in which the line "let's tend to the forests like prophets" reflects the importance of stewardship, cultural preservation, and environmental regeneration from an Indigenous perspective?

CONNECTING TO COMMUNITY: PROMPTS FOR LEARNING CIRCLES

❯ Beginning

- Share a teaching or lesson you have learned related to caring for the land.

- Imagine how your ancestors would have lived.

❯ Bridging

- Share an experience of a time when you guarded, protected, or defended someone or something and how you did this.

- Discuss how you might act differently if it was your responsibility to raise forests.

● **Beyond**
- Share some other environmental issues that this poem reminds you of.

- Discuss the experiences that might inspire someone to become a water walker, land defender, prophet, or Land Guardian or Watchman.

CONNECTING TO LAND-BASED LEARNING

❭ **Beginning**
- Create "seed balls" using dirt, compost, clay, and seeds native to your area. Place (or throw!) these seed balls around the school neighbourhood to revitalize native plants in forests, school yards, boulevards, and more.

- If you've had an opportunity to take a walk in an old-growth forest, share your memory of this, or look at old-growth forests online. Spend time searching for the oldest trees in your local area. Look into how old these trees might be and how they have been protected for long enough to reach that age. You may be able to find evidence in archives of stories documenting humans coming to their defence.

❭ **Bridging**
- Collaborate with local environmental organizations to plan a forest restoration project. Participate in activities such as clearing invasive species, planting native trees, and maintaining trails.

- Collaborate with other students and local organizations or Knowledge Keepers to create maps of a local forest, noting important landmarks, plant species, and wildlife habitats. Discuss the value of mapping in land management.

● **Beyond**

- Practise the act of stillness. Use the following quotation as inspiration: "Instead of going into the forest to observe it, we also need to sit and let it observe us."[3]

- Read and analyze a news story about people trying to protect old-growth forests from logging. Map the opposing arguments that are found in the story.

CONNECTING TO LAND BACK

- The Mi'kmaq territory (in Atlantic Canada) is unceded and is part of a Peace and Friendship Treaty signed in 1726.[4] The Land Back movement asks us to consider how long it would take to restore the land to its original inhabitants or renew it to its pre-colonial state. Reflect on the historical injustices mentioned in "Raising Forests." These include deforestation and the refusal to allow L'nu hunters entry to their own territory, which forced disconnections from "their livelihoods and continuity." According to the Indigenous Law Association at McGill, "Honouring family relations, *msit no'kmaq* (all my relations), is vital to Mi'kmaq daily life, guiding individual and collective interactions and their relations with the universe. It is the framework of their constitution. The Mi'kmaq believe that the spirits of their ancestors reside in the land, sea and sky. They take seriously their responsibility to honour and protect the legacies of their ancestors for future generations."[5] How have historical injustices like those described in "Raising Forests" impacted Indigenous communities, and how have the communities persevered? What actions can you take to assist in restoring and renewing the land?

---

3   Frank Meuse, quoted by shalan joudry, in "How Being Still in Nature Can Remind Us of What It Means to Be Human," CBC News, May 29, 2020, www.cbc.ca/news/canada/nova-scotia/shalan-joudry-nature -mi-kmaw-storyteller-ecologist-1.5590273.

4   Government of Canada, Fact Sheet on Peace and Friendship Treaties in the Maritimes and Gaspé, www.rcaanc-cirnac.gc.ca/eng/1100100028599/1539609517566. For more information, see Dr. Sherry Pictou, "Mi'kmaq and the Recognition and Implementation of Rights Framework," Yellowhead Institute, June 5, 2018, yellowheadinstitute.org/2018/06/05/mikmaq-rights-framework/.

5   Jane McMillan, "Rooted in Mi'kma'ki: Living L'nu Constitutionalism," Indigenous Law Association at McGill, indigenous-law-association-at-mcgill.com/2021/06/03/rooted-in-mikmaki-living-lnu -constitutionalism/.

CONNECTIONS TO OTHER INDIGENOUS RESOURCES

Books

Birdsong, by Julie Flett (Greystone Books, 2019; ages 3–8).
This picture book shares the story of a young girl who feels lonely and out of place after moving to a new town. It focuses on building new relationships, with connections to seasonal changes, life and death, and the cycles of the moon.

The Bee Mother, by Hetxw'ms Gyetxw (Brett D. Huson) (HighWater Press, 2024; ages 9–12).
Part of the Mothers of Xsan series, this book shows the bee life cycle from the perspective of a mother bee on Gitxsan territory, and makes strong connections to the science curriculum.

The Winona LaDuke Chronicles: Stories from the Front Lines in the Battle for Environmental Justice, by Winona LaDuke (Fernwood, 2017).
This book shares inspirational stories of Indigenous environmental activism from across the continent.

Films

Kanehsatake: 270 Years of Resistance, directed by Alanis Obomsawin (National Film Board, 1993). <www.nfb.ca/film/kanehsatake_270_years_of_resistance/>. This documentary covers the time Obomsawin spent filming the armed standoff between protestors, the police, and the Canadian army that arose from a dispute over a proposed golf course to be built on Kanien'kehá:ka (Mohawk) lands.

Online

"How Being Still in Nature Can Remind Us of What It Means to Be Human," by shalan joudry, CBC News, May 29, 2020. <www.cbc.ca/news/canada /nova-scotia/shalan-joudry-nature-mi-kmaw-storyteller-ecologist -1.5590273>.
In this audio essay accompanied by written text, shalan joudry shares her thoughts on the importance of being in and connecting to nature.

Indigenous Environmental Network. <www.ienearth.org/>.
This is a grassroots organization based in the US. The website includes links, resources, and radio livestreams; it offers ideas for mobilizing climate

justice, environmental issues, sustainability, and the ongoing protection of health, land, water, air, and sacred sites.

"Staring Down the Precipice," by shalan joudry, Cedar Meuse-Waterman, and Rose Meuse, CBC. <newsinteractives.cbc.ca/longform/staring-down -the-precipice>.
This multi-voiced essay shares the perspectives of three women on their journey of learning to speak Mi'kmaw.

Whose Land. <www.whose.land/en/>.
This is an important website for all teachers living and working in Canada. It supports work acknowledging traditional and treaty territories, including the locations and names of Indigenous communities and reminders of where residential schools were located. It also provides stories of Indigenous leadership and valuable teaching resources and lesson guides.

Indigenous Guardians Program. <www.indigenousguardianstoolkit.ca /chapter/get-know-toolkit>.
This site provides information about the Indigenous Guardians who monitor, manage, and steward their lands and waters. It describes how to implement, get involved in, or manage a program based on the Indigenous Guardianship model or support protection of lands and waters through other actions.

Podcast
Trails, Tales, and Spruce Tea, hosted by shalan joudry and Frank Meuse. <www.shalanjoudry.com/podcasts>.
This podcast focuses on Mi'kmaw life, featuring powerful casual conversations and stories connected to land.

Michif Language Revitalization

Our Lessons On-line and On-land

TRICIA LOGAN is Assistant Professor in First Nations and Indigenous Studies and cross-appointed to the School of Public Policy and Global Affairs at the University of British Columbia. She is a Métis scholar with more than 20 years of experience working with Indigenous communities in Canada and has held roles at the National Centre for Truth and Reconciliation, the Canadian Museum for Human Rights, the Métis Centre at the National Aboriginal Health Organization, the Aboriginal Healing Foundation, and the Legacy of Hope Foundation.

———

OVER THE LAST 20 YEARS, I have worked with Survivors of residential schools and histories of Métis attendance at residential school. I have repeatedly turned to language learning as a method of working in partnership with Survivors and their stories, and as a personal and shared response to processing these experiences. There is a clear connection between listening to residential school experiences, processing trauma histories of the schools, and confronting those histories by relearning and revitalizing Indigenous languages.[1] Residential schools in Canada were created and operated with the clear goal of forcibly removing Indigenous languages, knowledges, and cultural teachings from generations of families,

---

1   Lorena Fontaine, "Redress for Linguicide: Residential Schools and Assimilation in Canada," *British Journal of Canadian Studies* 30, no. 2 (2017): 184.

which included taking children from their home territories, lands, waters, and kinship systems.[2]

I often learn and relearn just how well language brings us back home, to any territory we consider home, and in whatever form home takes. In this essay, I will describe my own experiences with land and language.

I grew up in a rural home in Northwestern Ontario. I didn't imagine then how urbanized I would become in my adult years. Now I live in Vancouver, British Columbia, far from my homes near Thunder Bay, Ontario, and in Manitoba. The territories and land I live on today belong to the Musqueam Nation. As a visitor here, the teachings, knowledge, and stories tied to this land are new to me. Language learning has helped me find connections to this territory and feel less disconnected in a "foreign" city. Some of the first words of hən'q'əmin'əm' language that I learned were local place names in Vancouver; these often refer to the trees, land, and rivers. As an Indigenous language learner, my first instinct is to translate new terms into my own Indigenous language rather than to English, and to tie them back to where I come from. The words for *cedar*, *river*, *wind*, *rushing water*, and *medicines* were among the first words I learned, and I tried to translate them to Michif, rather than English.

Didaan aen nipinet, nii kinaahk.
In the spruce. My home.
(Image courtesy of Tricia Logan.)

---

2   Truth and Reconciliation Commission of Canada, *Honouring the Truth, Reconciling for the Future: Summary of the Final Report of the Truth and Reconciliation Commission of Canada* (McGill-Queen's University Press), 153–54.

Over 10 years ago, I took part in a Mentor-Apprentice Program (MAP) for language learning and revitalization. I lived in full language immersion with two Michif speakers, Elders Rita Flamand and Grace Zoldy, for a summer. My home was a small cabin on the shores of Lake Winnipegosis, and the lake, land, territory, and waters were built into the immersion teachings.

The program meets both the mentor (teacher) and apprentice (learner) *where* they are in their language journey, their day-to-day lives, and their location.[3] Teachers and learners use their own homes, community gathering spaces, and all kinds of locations on the land, including in the bush, gardens, berry patches, and ceremonial spaces. The immersion often involves walks, visiting, and running errands to develop vocabulary and practise conversations. Pedagogical design originates from kinship and language. Teaching and "lessons" are not forced into the learning; they almost always arrive in the context of where participants are and what they are doing.

The difficult times stemming from the pandemic that began in 2020 provided me with a chance to relearn language online. I confronted the reality that I am a use-it-or-lose-it language learner; without continuity in my lessons, my language fluency quickly fades. I was forgetting much of the Michif I had learned a decade earlier. Online language classes provided by advocate-teacher Heather Souter in Camperville, Manitoba, in 2020–2021 built what was needed during those times: a language community. Each morning, we would use our phrases to ask each other "How are you feeling?" which had more gravity during pandemic times. We shared our homes, our pets—*lii minoush pii lii kwashoon* (cats and pigs)—and gave one another a reason to stay engaged, describing what the land looked like outside our respective windows.

To confront both language continuity and the importance of forming a speaking community, my colleague, Michif language classmate, and friend Ashley Edwards (a new Michif speaker like me) began creating social media image-language posts. She would post an image and label it with a short Michif phrase, simultaneously increasing the visibility of Michif language,

---

3   The Mentor-Apprentice Program is highly adaptable as an Indigenous-led learning and teaching method that has dedicated connections to teachings tied to culture and land. See Leanne Hinton et al., "The Master-Apprentice Language Learning Program," in *The Routledge Handbook of Language Revitalization*, ed. Leanne Hinton, Leena Huss, and Gerald Roche (Routledge, 2018), 128–29.

practising her conversational language skills, connecting beauty, language, and land, and building community. Her approach resonated with me, and I started to create my own posts a couple of times a week. As the members of the language classes and study groups were "calling in" from different locations, we used social media to build relationality and ties to the land online because they could not be built in person. Once a week, we joined an online Michif card game, hosted by language teacher and advocate Kai Pyle. Kai invited new learners to the online space, contributing new vocabularies and methodologies. The communal generosity of Michif teachers and fellow speakers extends beyond pedagogy and outreach. Métis family visiting, kinship, teachings, and our virtual tie to our home communities may be a reimagined future, but it may also be an adapted society. Métis have continuous diasporic affiliations to their communities. These adaptations are a classic Métis tactic: using the best of what is available and adapting it for Métis-specificity.[4]

The images shared here were part of our social media posts, our short conversations, and our daily language touchpoints. They were part of our ongoing conversations, often representing a way of spelling out and repeating some of the vocabulary we'd learned that day. They allowed us to step out of our busy-ness and step back into language. They were part of how we reconnected to land and teachings. Whether or not they are overtly or consciously connected to a confrontation with capitalism, hegemony, or colonialism, our walks, our rests, and our return to language is our way to revive.[5] These social media posts often emerged from our walks as Métis in Coast Salish territories, picking the berries of the Pacific, finding the recipes of our homes, and meeting "in the middle" to support each other in how we have defined a land-language learning environment as *lii fii Michif*.

---

4 Lindsay Nixon, "Visual Cultures of Indigenous Futurism," in *Otherwise Worlds: Against Settler-Colonialism and Anti-Blackness*, ed. Tiffany Lethabo King, Jenell Navarro, and Andrea Smith (Duke University Press, 2020), 333.

5 Sofia Steinvorth, "Rest as Resistance: From Self-Care to Decolonial Narratives," in *Cultures of Silence*, ed. Luísa Santos (Routledge, 2022), 157.

Didaan lii graan cayd
ki-pimohtaanaan.
We are walking in
the big cedars.
(Image courtesy of Tricia Logan.)

I remain at a beginner-novice level in my language learning, and I am slowly building and retaining a vocabulary. But I must remember to take a step back to see what else is being built alongside this: the importance of building community through language learning, as both a methodology and as an outcome, cannot be overstated. Many Métis people and Michif speakers face diasporic disconnection from their own home territories, lands, waters, teachings, and resources. Social, political, geographic, historic, and economic barriers make it difficult for some individuals to "connect" to their territories.[6] Child-welfare systems and structures of assimilation, like residential schools, that attempted to sever kinship and language ties to the land continue to make access to traditional lands and territories difficult. For many, language helps recreate or reimagine the connections we cannot always make in person.

---

6   Renée Monchalin, Janet Smylie, and Cheryllee Bourgeois, "'It's Not Like I'm More Indigenous There and I'm Less Indigenous Here': Urban Métis Women's Identity and Access to Health and Social Services in Toronto, Canada," *AlterNative: An International Journal of Indigenous Peoples* 16, no. 4 (2020): 323–31.

Educator Connections

Read the editors' thoughts and engage in reflection. Respond to the questions that follow on your own or with your colleague(s).

PERSONAL CONNECTIONS

Christine: While reading Tricia Logan's essay, I was brought back to my own experience of trying to keep students engaged and build community online during the COVID-19 pandemic. During this time I was also working on a contract with the Manitoba Indigenous Cultural Education Centre's Anishinaabemowin language-learning program, and I had the opportunity to sit in and observe some online language classes. The language teachers included Patricia Ningewance, Dennis Chartrand, and the late Roger Roulette. It was fascinating to see the way these mentor educators adapted their programs for the online space, ensuring that community was centred. They facilitated introductions and role-playing and improv games—all in the Anishinaabemowin language. Like Tricia Logan, I am still a beginning learner in my traditional language, but I value the community-building aspect of language just as much as the language building (and maybe more!).

Katya: While I am not fluent in my ancestral languages, hearing people speak these languages makes me feel closer to home, and somehow even closer to family members who are no longer with us on Earth. I really admire Tricia Logan's determination and creativity in continuing to learn and connect to land and community during the pandemic. Her photos are a great reminder to connect language learning to land. They share actions of the everyday and show us that language is everywhere. When practising reading the Michif words and phrases alongside the photos, I needed to use many strategies—the visual connections, the translations, and the repetitive practise—to get the words to flow. This illustrates the complex process of language learning and the value of community for practise and support.

- How does your teaching "meet both the mentor (teacher) and apprentice (learner) *where* they are in their journey, their day-to-day lives, and their location"?

- To what extent does your own pedagogical design "originate from kinship and language"? How might you expand on this concept in your own practice?

- What are some strategies you use to keep students engaged when teaching online?

- What aspects of your own practice serve as a "confrontation with capitalism, hegemony, or colonialism"?

- Look into the vocabulary of different languages to describe the natural environment around your school. Create a multilingual resource that names trees, shrubs, flowers, seeds, animals, and other aspects of nature in multiple languages, including a local Indigenous language.

- Look up language-learning opportunities in your local area. What languages are represented? Are there languages present in your community that are not represented in language-learning settings?

- As a school team, think about the types of language-learning approaches you take. How can you include more connections to the land in language instruction?

- Look at the information provided within the school (on posters, signage, etc.). How can you make more languages visible and accessible when sharing information?

Classroom Connections

Introduce to students the narrative and the Connected Concepts you wish to focus on. Use the following questions, prompts, and resource suggestions to guide student learning.

CONNECTED CONCEPTS

- Language revitalization
- Connecting online
- Homeland

CONNECTING TO SELF: PROMPTS FOR PERSONAL REFLECTION

❭ Beginning

- What languages do you speak?

- What languages do your family members or the adults around you speak? What languages have been spoken in your family throughout the generations?

❭ Bridging

- How does the language you hear at home make you feel?

- How can words be helpful? How can words be harmful?

● Beyond

- What makes you feel connected to your ancestors? What makes you feel disconnected from them?

- What is your preferred way to build community?

- When have you felt that something meaningful was "lost in translation"?

CONNECTING TO COMMUNITY: PROMPTS FOR LEARNING CIRCLES

❭ Beginning

- Share some words or phrases you know in another language and how you learned them.

- Describe the language teachers in your life.

❭ Bridging

- Share your thoughts on the "use-it-or-lose-it" language-learning experience that Tricia Logan describes.

Beyond

- Describe what "homeland" means to you.

- Share some of the connections between language and kinship in your own family.

CONNECTING TO LAND-BASED LEARNING

) Beginning

- What are some of the first words that are important to know when learning a new language? Are any of these words connected to land?

- Learn a few words in a local Indigenous language. Practise the correct pronunciation.

) Bridging

- Look at local place names in Indigenous languages and try, as Tricia Logan did, to "tie them back to where [you] come from." For example, many Indigenous place names describe the local landscape.

- Take images of the land, like the ones shared here by Tricia Logan, and write dual-language captions for them.

Beyond

- Tricia Logan writes, "As a visitor here, the teachings, knowledge, and stories tied to this land are new to me." Take a walk to look for the lessons you want to learn from the land.

- What are some words or phrases connected to the land? In what ways do they connect to the land? Are any of these words or phrases in other languages?

CONNECTING TO LAND BACK

- Language programming and revitalization are actions that contribute and connect to the Land Back movement: language back, land back. Disconnections from land and home territories changed the way Indigenous languages were used and preserved. The Truth and Reconciliation

Commission of Canada acknowledges that removals from land and concentrated efforts to compel people to "only speak English" have had effects on language loss, and calls 13 to 17 of the TRC's Calls to Action address strengthening access to learning Indigenous languages. Explore these Calls to Action and select one that is relevant to your school. Determine if your school is adequately addressing that Call to Action. What can you do to advocate for its full adoption or to help amplify the presence of Indigenous languages in your school or community?

- There have been some historic situations where land has been returned as a result of reconciliatory efforts; for example, Batoche, in Saskatchewan, is the site of the historic Battle of Batoche, which took place in 1885 between the Métis and the Canadian government. Can you find another example of a place where Métis land has been restored or where Métis communities have been compensated for land theft? For example, check out the story of Ste. Madeleine, which involved the transfer of approximately 100 acres of Crown land to the Manitoba Métis Federation.[7]

CONNECTIONS TO OTHER INDIGENOUS RESOURCES
Books
Berry Song, by Michaela Goade (Little, Brown Books for Young Readers, 2022; ages 4–8).
This picture book is about intergenerational connections to and appreciation for land.

On the Trapline, by David A. Robertson (Tundra Books, 2021; ages 4–8).
This award-winning picture book connects to Indigenous land practices on the trapline and relationships to land through a dialogue between a boy and his moshom. Gentle connections are interwoven between living and learning together on the land versus learning in school.

---

7   Darren Bernhardt, "Historic Agreement to See Ste. Madeleine Land Returned to Manitoba Métis," CBC News, July 19, 2024, www.cbc.ca/news/canada/manitoba/ste-madeleine-manitoba-métis-land-transfer-1.7268948.

Stolen Words, by Melanie Florence (Second Story Press, 2017; ages 6–9).
This book connects to the theme of language loss due to the intergenerational impacts of residential schools in an accessible way for younger audiences.

Wâpikwaniy: A Beginner's Guide to Métis Floral Beadwork, by Gregory Scofield and Amy Briley (Gabriel Dumont Institute, 2011).
A practical guide to beginning Métis beadwork and historical connections. Supports the idea that language learning is embedded within cultural practices.

Online

Manitoba Indigenous Cultural Education Centre. <www.micec.com/>.
The MICEC is a non-profit organization that aims to revitalize Indigenous languages in Manitoba. The site offers language-learning resources, including games and videos.

"'We Will Get This Land Back': Métis Displaced for Cattle Want to Rebuild Their Community," Global News, July 17, 2023. <globalnews.ca /video/9838668/we-will-get-this-land-back-metis-displaced-for-cattle -want-to-rebuild-their-community>.
This news story describes how hundreds of Métis community members are advocating for their land to be returned.

"Freedom"

DAKOTA BEAR is a Treaty 6 Cree hip-hop artist, activist, and clothing designer. His melodic rhymes carry stories of Indigenous Peoples across Canada, leaving listeners enlightened and inspired by his music and message. His work with Idle No More, Missing and Murdered Indigenous Women, Girls, and Two-Spirit Peoples, and the Global Climate Strike has intertwined his music with international social justice movements and connected him with fans across the country.

———

THIS SONG is a potent cry for justice, equality, and liberty, touching upon the trials and tribulations endured by Indigenous communities in North America due to suppression and marginalization. I released the music video for "Freedom" to extend a hand of solidarity.

The lyrics of "Freedom" mirror a deep-rooted sense of togetherness and grit among us, as we unite against the adversities and learn to work through the hurdles thrown our way. In the lyrics, I speak of a pledge made to us, assuring us that our struggles will bear fruit, shedding light on the hopeful and resolute message the song carries.

Freedom

The people are standing together
There's power in numbers
We will not fall where you want us
We learning the laws you throwin' upon us
You throw us in water, we know there's piranhas
The people, they needing a leader, just know that I'm on it
I'm honest in everything that I do
Every word that I write is true
The people that get it, they know that the picture is bigger
So pull up a seat and you'll listen
You putting your fist in the air, you know the resistance is here
You hear us off in the distance
We are the kids that you dismissed
We are the targets you just missed
We are descendants of healers and chiefs
Just know that our struggles are brief
Just know that we one and the same
I'm from the prairies, the plains
I'll grow my hair out until I can braid it again
I'm no longer ashamed
I promised our people our hardships shall not go in vain
You're hearing my voice and the melody carry the pain
I do not do this for money or fame
I just wanna be me
I just wanna feel free
Is that too much that we ask?
Look to the future, we'll learn from the past
I know that sometimes we clash
And that's just life
Chances ain't handed out twice
A man of my word and a man of advice
I just wanna feel free

We just wanna live our lives
We don't wanna have to worry

Tell me, can you help me?
It don't seem like you been in a hurry
You playin' judge and jury
I feel I'm under siege
Get the matches, burn the sage
Chapter's over, turn the page
Author of my destiny, but they tellin' me differently
We just wanna live our lives
We don't wanna have to worry
Tell me, can you help me?
It don't seem like you been in a hurry
I just wanna be me
I just wanna feel free

I swear we been doin' the most
I'll pack my suitcase and move to the coast
I promise that next time I come to this city, I'm bringin' hope
I'm bringin' you and it's bigger than music
Together we started a movement
Together we stand
We shakin' the earth as we move
And as soon as you look for the answer you see the solution
Our minds are as clear as the water as soon as you see the pollution
We want the freedom and not the illusion
We are the warriors
The ones that you read in the stories
We are notorious
I just wanna be me
I just wanna feel free

We just wanna live our lives
We don't wanna have to worry
Tell me, can you help me?
It don't seem like you been in a hurry
You playin' judge and jury

I feel I'm under siege
Get the matches, burn the sage
Chapter's over, turn the page
Author of my destiny, but they tellin' me differently
We just wanna live our lives
We don't wanna have to worry
Tell me, can you help me?
It don't seem like you been in a hurry
I just wanna be me
I just wanna feel free

Educator Connections

Read the editors' thoughts and engage in reflection. Respond to the questions that follow on your own or with your colleague(s).

PERSONAL CONNECTIONS

Christine: I love this song. I had the honour of working with Dakota Bear on Your Voice is Power, a hip-hop coding program aimed at promoting social justice while teaching youth about coding and computer science. He is one of our artist partners, and we analyze this song in the curriculum (which is available free of charge at www.yourvoiceispower.ca). I've witnessed him perform this song in front of audiences of all Indigenous students and all non-Indigenous students, and the reception is always the same: students are inspired by his words, honesty, story, and commitment to uplifting Indigenous people. The video for this song was shot at an Idle No More rally, which demonstrates Dakota's commitment to spreading the message of Indigenous stewardship and self-determination. Play this song for students—they will love it!

Katya: I read this song like a poem, and then when I watched the music video, it really came to life. Dakota Bear's strength and skills shine through. The rhythm, the rhymes, and the repetition all work to convey a message of resistance. When he says the words "We are the kids that you dismissed / We are the targets you just missed," it sounds like he is speaking directly to teachers; this reminds me of my particular responsibilities as a teacher. I listened to this song over and over. Each time I listened and watched the video, new words stood out. How do we create learning environments where kids can be themselves and free themselves? What and whom have I missed or dismissed?

EDUCATOR INQUIRY AND ACTIONS

- What do you think the message of "Freedom" conveys about the struggles and aspirations of Indigenous Peoples? How does this message relate to broader social justice movements?

- Has this song shifted your perspective on the importance of music and visual and performing arts as vehicles for advocacy and storytelling, particularly within Indigenous communities? If so, how?

- What are some ways in which the lyrics of "Freedom" reflect themes of unity, resilience, and empowerment among Indigenous youth?

- Discuss some of the obstacles to achieving justice, equality, and liberty for Indigenous communities, as portrayed in the song. How can these obstacles be addressed through education and awareness?

- How can educators and schools support Indigenous youth activists like Dakota Bear and amplify their voices in working toward social justice and environmental activism?

- Dakota Bear writes, "We are the warriors / The ones that you read in the stories / We are notorious." Reflect on these lyrics in relation to your own teaching. How can educators inspire students to explore and celebrate the rich history and contributions of Indigenous Peoples?

- As a school team, consider how you can integrate Indigenous perspectives, histories, and voices, as exemplified by Dakota Bear's music, into your curriculum and educational programs. How can you foster a learning environment that promotes social justice and equity for all students?

Classroom Connections

Introduce to students the lyrics and the Connected Concepts you wish to focus on. Use the following questions, prompts, and resource suggestions to guide student learning.

CONNECTED CONCEPTS

- Idle No More
- Sovereignty
- Activism
- Self-determination

CONNECTING TO SELF: PROMPTS FOR PERSONAL REFLECTION

❯ Beginning

- Listen to the song "Freedom." What do you think of the lyrics and beat?

- Have you ever stood up for something you believed in? What was it?

❯ Bridging

- What does the concept of "freedom" mean to you? What do you think it means to Dakota Bear?

- Was there a particular time when you felt connected to a community? Consider why you felt this way.

- How do you like to express yourself (e.g., through speaking, writing, art)? Why do you like to express yourself in this way?

● Beyond

- What social justice issues are you passionate about? What are some ways you can advocate for, educate others about, or support a movement?

- Think about how art and music can be powerful tools for social change. Can you think of other art forms that have influenced social movements?

CONNECTING TO COMMUNITY: PROMPTS FOR LEARNING CIRCLES

❭ Beginning

- Share your favourite type of music and how it makes you feel.

- Share your favourite line from the song "Freedom" and explain why you chose it.

❭ Bridging

- Share a time when you felt free, describing where you were and who you were with.

- Find a poetic line in the song and try to identify some of the literary devices used in that line.

● Beyond

- Share a social justice movement that you are passionate about and why.

- The song is entitled "Freedom." After considering the lyrics, share what you think Dakota Bear wants freedom from.

CONNECTING TO LAND-BASED LEARNING

❭ Beginning

- Create a spoken word poem or short song inspired by the sounds and rhythms heard in your local environment. What message do you want to convey using the power of your voice?

- Take a walk in your local neighbourhood and look for messages of hope or activism, or calls for freedom and self-determination for people, plants, or animals. These messages could be in the form of, for example, a billboard, graffiti, or a plant growing through concrete.

❭ Bridging

- Participate in a social justice cause connected to the topic of land (e.g., protecting the land, land rights, land access) by volunteering for or attending a community event.

- Share a message of solidarity with a social justice cause connected to the topic of land in your territory.

● **Beyond**
- Research local Indigenous land rights or claims in your area. Brainstorm ways to support movements advocating for these issues.

- What land-related social justice issue do you feel needs to be addressed, and why? Start your own social justice movement by advocating for a relevant local issue connected to land reclamation, sovereignty, ecological justice, or language or cultural rights. Create a social media awareness campaign for taking action in your community.

CONNECTING TO LAND BACK

- Dakota Bear's "Freedom" is directly related to the Land Back movement. He surfaces tensions between past and present through issues of internalized oppression and carrying pain or shame in the present because of past injustices. In the line "Author of my destiny, but they tellin' me differently," he exposes the disconnections between those calling for freedom and existing power structures. He talks back to colonial systems when he raps, "We are the kids that you dismissed / We are the targets you just missed," which is particularly relevant to the education system. He has protested with Idle No More, and like that movement, through powerful repetition, this song encourages determined steps toward justice. On Dakota Bear's website <www.dakotabear.ca>, you can find more connections that show how he works toward freedom.

    Think about how various art forms can be used to educate about and raise awareness of the Land Back movement, including examples from this text. Select your favourite medium and create a work that takes action. How does your art advocate for the protection and conservation of land near your school or neighbourhood?

CONNECTIONS TO OTHER INDIGENOUS RESOURCES

Books

Nibi's Water Song, by Sunshine Tenasco (North Winds Press, 2019; ages 4–8). In this picture book about the power we have to create change, an Indigenous girl inspires the government to make clean water available to everyone.

Rock Your Mocs, by Laurel Goodluck (Heartdrum, 2023; ages 4–8). This playful and informative picture book depicts children from different nations being proud of their Indigeneity. Includes a pronunciation guide and an information page about traditional footwear and Rock Your Mocs Day, which began in 2011.

The Fox Wife, by Beatrice Deer (Inhabit Media, 2019; ages 6–8). This graphic-novel interpretation of a traditional Inuit story is based on a song by the author. It can help students see the connections between songs and stories and multiple literacies.

Maakusie Loves Music, by Jaaji and Chelsey June of Twin Flames (Arvaaq Press, 2022; ages 7–9). This picture book follows a young boy as he explores traditional and modern dance and music in the North.

The Eagle Feather Story, by Francois Prince (4Canoes, 2020). This dual-language (Dakelh and English) picture book for all ages features an ancient Dakelh (Carrier Peoples) story about learning to respect others, and the Earth itself.

Notable Native People: 50 Indigenous Leaders, Dreamers, and Changemakers from Past and Present, by Adrienne Keene (Ten Speed Press, 2021). This illustrated book for older readers profiles 50 notable American Indian, Alaska Native, and Native Hawaiian people, including leaders in education, arts, sports, and government.

Online

Resources for Rethinking. <resources4rethinking.ca/en/resource/water-is-life>.

This comprehensive website includes resources to support activism related to water that have been curated by teachers for teachers. Resources include aspects of assessment, sustainability education principles, and the pedagogical approaches used.

Podcast

"Black and Native Folks in the Climate Justice Movement," *Who Belongs?*, Episode 39. <belonging.berkeley.edu/podcast-black-and-native-folks-climate-justice-movement>.

This episode focuses on Black and Indigenous connections to addressing the climate crisis. The founding members of The Wind & The Warrior, a community that combines social activism and spiritual practice, describe their pilgrimage along the Mississippi River.

Manitou Akiing/
Spirit Is in the Land
An Urban Land-Based Education
Program Within Human Ecology

SHIRLI EWANCHUK is from Swan Lake First Nation in Manitoba. As a Bear Clan member, her main responsibilities are understanding and working with ceremony, plant medicines, and the creation of healing spaces, while also undertaking peacekeeping and reconciliation work. She has worked alongside First Nations people at the community, tribal, and political levels, allowing her to connect to, form relationships with, and learn from community Knowledge Keepers. Shirli has created 30 health, healing, and education programs, and plans to continue creating such initiatives.

HOW DID THE MANITOU AKIING PROGRAM GET STARTED?

I had the great fortune of teaching Indigenous Human Ecology at Opask-wayak Cree Nation and Peguis First Nation. I was encouraged and given the leeway to create my own curricula for these two reserve communities. Later, while I was creating the Ojibwe Language and Culture Program for the Louis Riel School Division (LRSD) in Winnipeg, I carried this knowledge forward as I approached the superintendent with a proposal to create an Indigenous Land-Based Human Ecology Program. In September 2020, I received approval and support to work in earnest on developing this program.

I believe that Human Ecology classrooms and teachers are underutilized resources for teaching land-based education. Here's why: Human Ecology classrooms usually have kitchen setups, allowing teaching on Indigenous foods and gardening to be brought from outside into the classroom. They offer sewing machines and hand tools to create hand-tanned leathers from the four-leggeds, birds, and fish, and beautiful traditional and cultural clothing and items to ensure the continuance of Indigenous knowledge. Family studies classes provide opportunities to teach traditional Indigenous parenting, clans, and kinship teachings and demonstrate their connections to the land.

I was inspired to create this program because transferring the knowledge of living on the land and being able to survive is paramount to keeping ourselves, our children, and the ones yet to be born alive. How will we survive if we don't know how to hunt, fish, trap, harvest, build, find clean water, and clothe ourselves? Living in the city can disconnect you from the natural world. The Manitou Akiing Program helps build connection to the land for both teachers and students.

WHAT WERE THE STEPS IN DEVELOPING THE MANITOU AKIING PROGRAM?

During the first year of program development I did an environmental scan of the high schools in the LRSD to learn about their outside environments, identifying the trees, plants, rivers, streams, and outside spaces at each school. I also performed a literature review for existing programs similar to the one I wanted to create; unfortunately, I couldn't find any Indigenous land-based Human Ecology programs. So, I set about to build the bike as I rode it, as our superintendent says.

In the fall of 2020, while completing the environmental scans and literature review, I attended an online talk about pictographs and petroglyphs. The presenter shared Midewiwin teachings on a particular glyph known as the Four Axes that was left by the Elders/Knowledge Keepers just after the ice sheets had melted thousands of years ago. Through these guide markings of axes, carved into and then painted on stone, our ancestors tell us what we need to teach our children: how to build, hunt, plant, and harvest. These four essential skills ensure that our children and their children have the knowledge needed to survive on the land. This teaching is the basis of the Manitou Akiing Program.

As another step in setting up the program, I conducted a curriculum review of all Human Ecology courses in Manitoba's provincial curriculum to determine where links to Indigenous teachings and knowledge could be made. I assessed the resources and supplies I would need to purchase and created a list of people who carry specific skills for surviving and thriving on the land. No one person has every skill; to build the program, I needed to collaborate and build partnerships with other Knowledge Keepers.

WHAT KNOWLEDGE IS SHARED IN THE MANITOU AKIING PROGRAM?

Over the four years since the program began, I've designed several lessons each year, creating programming for grades 9 to 12. I've learned how to stagger the lessons to provide fresh knowledge for the students each year. This table shows the typical topics I cover in Human Ecology.

SUBJECT AREA	TOPICS
Clothing and Textiles	• Indigenous plants and dyes • hide tanning, leather work • harvesting seeds for beads; history of beads • caribou tufting, quill work, and gathering • Indigenous clothing styles • impact of fur trade/colonization/policies • right to hunt, trap, and clothe ourselves • how to hunt, trap, and snare • building shelters for thriving and surviving
Family Studies	• traditional Indigenous parenting • Indigenous Creation stories and sacred places • moss bag teachings; moss gathering • Indigenous family systems: Clans (star teachings), kinship, and societies • matriarchal structures in Manitoba • Indigenous midwifery; the birthing lodge • creating a parenting bundle • tipi setup and takedown; tipi teachings • Indigenous toys, stories, and games • household family medicine cabinet

Foods and Nutrition	• the Indigenous food basket • food security and food sovereignty • Indigenous foods, recipes, and test kitchens • hunting, fishing, and snaring rights; how to hunt, fish, and snare • Spirit plate, feasts • outdoor firepit cooking methods • Indigenous planting, harvesting, preserving, and storage practices • animal, fish, and bird life cycles and seasonality of food gathering
Geography	• Indigenous foods and migration patterns • Indigenous seed planting and gardening • cooking on the land and shelter building • the six seasons of food; little people offerings • neighbourhood tree and plant walks and teachings • storytelling for survival • food security and food sovereignty: treaty rights and responsibilities • sacredness of water and carrying the water • Circle of Life Turtle teachings, water teachings • enduring impacts of the Indian Act and other policies • renaissance of Indigenous food and gardens

I seek out and invite guest speakers, including fishers who bring us fresh fish and teach us to fillet them, a group to teach us hide tanning using traditional methods, and Indigenous midwives to help us understand the birthing experience.

I have created relationships with Human Ecology teachers, one high school at a time, creating relationships built on trust and mutual respect. I work alongside the teachers and their students to build each teacher's capacity and understanding of our ways. The students call me Ninoshe (Aunty) Shirli. Sometimes we are inside in the classroom and that is okay, but the preference is for being outdoors whenever possible. I love that the bundle of Indigenous Land-Based Human Ecology teachings I've spent 32 years gathering is being unpacked!

WHAT ARE SOME CHALLENGES OF THE MANITOU AKIING PROGRAM?

Sometimes I encounter moral, ethical, cultural, and spiritual dilemmas in my work. Many times, I have come to a crossroads over what to share, whether to share, and with whom to share. I work through this by talking with community Elders and Knowledge Keepers. For example, in consulting with Elders from Long Plain, it was determined that the non-Indigenous Human Ecology teachers I work with should not create Star Blankets because of the sacred knowledge connected to them. The Elders expressed their concern that this could be considered cultural appropriation. I listened to them, and do not transmit this knowledge out of respect.

As another example, I have a passion for learning about Indigenous gardening methods, seeds we historically saved and grew, and plant medicines, and I often receive inquiries about these topics as well as requests to support the Indigenous aspects of school gardens. Recently, in a family studies class, a student asked whether we had plant medicines for increasing the likelihood of pregnancy and for terminating pregnancy. I confirmed that we have plant medicine teachings on this, but did not share my specific knowledge. I've come to understand that there is a balance point for me in what I feel I can share and what is sacred knowledge needing protection.

WHAT IS THE FUTURE OF THE MANITOU AKIING PROGRAM?

To make this program possible and successful, I needed administrative and funding support from senior leadership. I've reached out to my administration to purchase special Indigenous handmade tools, hire guest speakers, and receive special training. I have an excellent support team, and Creator has been on my side too!

When you're operating a program—this includes teaching a course—I recommend that you continuously gather data. In my quest for program improvement, I've evaluated the Manitou Akiing Program as I go, using exit slips, discussions with classroom teachers, and formal student and teacher surveys, and now have a small but growing pool of data to draw on. In my baseline measurement in the first year, I discovered that only 17 percent of senior high school Human Ecology teachers were including Indigenous perspectives in their courses. After the third year of the Manitou Akiing Program, we are now at 50 percent program uptake. I view this as both an indicator of success and an indication of room to grow.

Through this sharing, I hope that you will see the potential for connecting Human Ecology to land-based learning, and that you too can create land-based learning opportunities. With more time and further strategic planning, I want to continue to build the Manitou Akiing Program. I hope to be working with all seven high school Human Ecology teams in LRSD next year, in what will be the fifth year of program development. I feel like I'm making an important contribution to our staff and students and to keeping the teachings I have been given alive. I really love what I do.

Educator Connections

Read the editors' thoughts and engage in reflection. Respond to the questions that follow on your own or with your colleague(s).

PERSONAL CONNECTIONS

Christine: I first met Shirli Ewanchuk in 2016 at the annual Medicine Eagle Camp in Keeseekoowenin First Nation, where the late Stella Blackbird was passing down knowledge related to traditional medicines. Shirli and I realized we had a connection—our families are both from Swan Lake First Nation. We've kept in touch ever since, and I had the opportunity to interview her about how she integrates land-based learning into her Human Ecology program. Even though I'm not a Human Ecology teacher, I'm inspired to incorporate some of the topics she covers into my English program, as well as to follow her lead by collaborating with Elders and Knowledge Keepers. I'm a huge fan of the work she does, so I'm excited that it is finally being shared—and I hope it serves as an inspiration to others.

Katya: This is inspiring work! Shirli Ewanchuk has put so many years of thinking and collaborating into the creation of the Manitou Akiing Program. I found it interesting that the inspiration for this curriculum emerged from imagery of the Four Axes of the ancient petroglyphs, outlining four key elements needed for future generations. There are so many practical elements laid out here that Shirli is generously sharing in order for people to learn from the work she is doing in Manitoba. Another standout element is the real-deal discussion about challenges in this work, which will provide helpful guidance for school and divisional teams as they continue or venture into similar curriculum work.

EDUCATOR INQUIRY AND ACTIONS

- Why do you think it's important to teach students traditional building, hunting, planting, and harvesting skills as part of Indigenous land-based education? How can hands-on activities related to shelter construction contribute to students' understanding of Indigenous survival skills?

- How can urban schools incorporate some of this type of land-based curriculum into their own programs?

- Has this essay shifted your perspective on the significance of building, hunting, planting, and harvesting skills in Indigenous culture? Reflect on the role of these skills in Indigenous communities and how it connects to self-sufficiency and resilience.

- What obstacles might educators encounter when implementing building, hunting, planting, and harvesting activities in their classrooms or in outdoor settings? Consider challenges related to safety, resource availability, and cultural sensitivity.

- The author writes, "No one person has every skill; to build the program, I needed to collaborate and build partnerships with other Knowledge Keepers." Reflect on this sentence in relation to your own teaching of land-based education skills. How can educators collaborate with local experts or community members to enhance students' learning experiences in this area?

- As a school team, how can you collectively support the integration of building, hunting, planting, and harvesting activities within your Indigenous land-based education program? Discuss strategies for curriculum development, leadership/mentorship, building on strengths and local knowledges, and creating safe and culturally respectful learning environments.

Classroom Connections

Introduce to students the narrative and the Connected Concepts you wish to focus on. Use the following questions, prompts, and resource suggestions to guide student learning.

CONNECTED CONCEPTS

- Clothing and textiles
- Food and nutrition
- Family studies
- Geography

CONNECTING TO SELF: PROMPTS FOR PERSONAL REFLECTION

) Beginning

- Which skill interests you the most: building, hunting, planting, or harvesting? Why is this of interest to you?

- Imagine you are an animal tracker. What animals might you find in your local area, and how could you learn about their habits and behaviours?

- If you could plant a garden, what types of foods would you choose to grow? Why do you think it's important to grow your own food?

- What do you know about the way your home is built, your food is planted, hunted, and harvested, or the way your clothing is made?

- Pick one of the Four Axes: building, hunting, planting, or harvesting. How does it connect to your prior knowledge?

● **Beyond**

- How might building, hunting, planting, and harvesting connect to Indigenous theories of sustainability?

- How might hunting be a sustainable practice?

CONNECTING TO COMMUNITY: PROMPTS FOR LEARNING CIRCLES

▶ **Beginning**

- Share which of the following skills interests you the most and explain why: building, hunting, planting, or harvesting.

- Share what you would build, plant, hunt, or harvest if you could choose anything. Explain why you would make this choice.

▶ **Bridging**

- Share an experience you have had with building, hunting, planting, or harvesting, and describe how it made you feel.

- Pick one of the Four Axes: building, hunting, planting, or harvesting. Share what you anticipate might be challenging for you.

● **Beyond**

- Share an Indigenous invention you know of or an Indigenous food you have tried.

- Shirli Ewanchuk shares an example of a practice that should not be used by non-Indigenous people. Choose one of the topics of study from the chart in Ewanchuk's essay, such as Indigenous clothing style, and discuss some other ways to avoid appropriation.

CONNECTING TO LAND-BASED LEARNING

❯ Beginning

- With guidance and in an appropriate location, learn how to safely build and start a fire. Consider taking this further by learning about different outdoor cooking methods.

- Look at the list of Human Ecology topics provided on pages 168–169, or research similar topics connected and relevant to your local territory. Choose one and map out the first steps you would need to take to investigate it. For example, if you chose to learn more about putting on a feast or want to cook outdoors, map out resources you might have or need and who you might ask for help.

❯ Bridging

- Go outside and look for animal tracks. Try to determine which animal created the tracks. Discuss animal behaviour and the importance of understanding wildlife.

- Participate in a guided foraging trip to identify and collect edible plants. Discuss the importance of responsible harvesting and respecting the land.

● Beyond

- Discuss the importance of shelter and its connections to Indigenous traditions. Design a shelter that can withstand various weather conditions. Determine and gather the materials you'll need and then build the shelter.

- Work with animal furs and leathers to create a piece of clothing. Reflect on how the process went and what you learned about Indigenous clothing.

CONNECTING TO LAND BACK

- In the Manitou Akiing Program, the name of the program, the topics studied, and the involvement of Elders and Knowledge Keepers are all ways to put land back into curricular and pedagogical practices. Reclaiming traditional Indigenous lifestyles and survival methods in an education system that was designed according to Eurocentric models that sought to disconnect people from land can create major tensions as land, culture, and language come to the forefront once again. How might the traditional activities included in the Manitou Akiing Program change over time? What new tools or materials could be used? Discuss the intersection of Indigenous inventions and contemporary challenges such as climate change and food insecurity. How can Indigenous knowledge inform solutions to these issues?

CONNECTIONS TO OTHER INDIGENOUS RESOURCES

Books

A Day with Yayah, by Nicola I. Campbell (Crocodile Books, 2017; ages 3–8). This picture book shows a First Nations grandmother teaching her granddaughter about edible plants and mushrooms.

Indigenous Ingenuity: A Celebration of Traditional North American Knowledge, by Deidre Havrelock and Edward Kay (Christy Ottaviano Books, 2023; ages 8–12).
This book highlights scientific discoveries and technological inventions by Indigenous North Americans, including advancements in the fields of transportation, communication, agriculture, medicines, sports, and more.

The Gift of the Little People (A Six Seasons of the Asiniskaw Ithiniwak Story), by William Dumas (HighWater Press, 2022; ages 9–11).
Set in the past, this story describes how a Rocky Cree boy saves his people from sickness and death with the help of the Little People.

Indigenous Community: Rekindling the Teachings of the Seventh Fire, by Gregory A. Cajete (Living Justice Press, 2015).
This book for adult readers focuses on community-building as a cultural and language revitalization method from a Tewa perspective. The author is an educator and scholar from Santa Clara Pueblo, New Mexico.

Land-Based Education Support Document for Educators (Manitoba First Nations Education Resource Centre, 2023).
This guide promotes land-based learning for schools and communities, including a wholistic focus on spiritual, emotional, mental, and physical elements.

Film

Spirit of the Trees: People of the Cedar, directed by Catherine Busch-Johnston, produced by Shannon Ramsay (National Film Board, 2008). <www.youtube.com/watch?v=JG9nJ1pybp8>.

This documentary features lessons about the importance of cedar as a life-sustaining gift. The Yakima share their concerns and philosophy on sustainable forestry and traditional food gathering.

Online

"3000-Year-Old Solutions to Modern Problems," by Lyla June, TEDxKC. <www.ted.com/talks/lyla_june_3000_year_old_solutions_to_modern _problems?language=en>.

Diné musician, scholar, and cultural historian Lyla June reframes Indigenous land-management practices as ancient solutions to modern problems.

"The Case for Recognizing Indigenous Knowledge as Science," by Albert Wiggan, TEDxSydney. <www.youtube.com/watch?v=FpJCYB_cCEQ>.

Australian environmental consultant Albert Wiggan explains why it is important to recognize Indigenous knowledge, especially in relation to climate change.

"Native American Representation in STEM: Indigenous Innovation," National Museum of the American Indian. <americanindian.si.edu/nk360 /informational/indigenous-innovation>.

This site lists culturally sensitive activities and resources for learning more about Indigenous scientific innovations.

Podcasts

Nihizhí, Our Voices: An Indigenous Solutions Podcast, hosted by Lyla June Johnston. <nihizhi.com/>.

This podcast provides conversations that centre Indigenous voices across Turtle Island, including those of grassroots innovators and organizers.

Think Indigenous, hosted by Ryan McMahon. <www.owltail.com/podcast /90321-Think-Indigenous>.

This podcast highlights keynotes and presentations from the annual Think Indigenous conference, sharing innovations and delivery models of Indigenous education.

PART FOUR

BECOMING

THIS SECTION PROMPTS US to think about learning as a process of *becoming* more aware of ourselves and our responsibilities within interconnected environments. We are encouraged to resist anthropocentric and Eurocentric tendencies. The contributors featured here remind us of the value of becoming more mindful of where and how we spend our time, and considering how our actions affect the Earth and all its inhabitants. As we learn from the diverse perspectives of Dan Henhawk (Kanien'kehá:ka), Réal Carrière (Nehinuw [Swampy Cree] and Métis), Hetxw'ms Gyetxw (Brett D. Huson) (Gitxsan), and Reanna McKay (Merasty) (Nîhithaw), creators whose homelands are on the West Coast, in the prairies, and in the regions just east of the Great Lakes, we enter into deeper relationship with land and water.

In his essay, Dan Henhawk encourages us to think about the connections between leisure and decolonization, writing about centring care for the environment rather than our own individual wants. He asks: "What would happen if we approached the world, and our own activities, with an understanding of our obligations as human beings to live in respectful relations with each other and with all our relations on the land, in the water, and throughout the cosmos?" (page 185). Questions like this help us reflect on Indigenous ways of being and doing and seek new ways of becoming attuned to our responsibilities beyond ourselves.

Réal Carrière reminds us that embracing Indigenous ways of knowing, being, doing, and becoming can begin with the simple yet profound act of listening. Carrière states, "Listen to my words and to what is in your heart. If you want to understand what land-based education is, you must take time to stop and reflect on what you are trying to do with your land-based education" (page 194). As you read this section, consider what land-based education means to you and how it could have a positive impact on the well-being of both you and your students. In addition, think of how it might affect your sense of responsibility to them.

From Hetxw'ms Gyetxw (Brett D. Huson), we learn about the land and words of wisdom—yuhlim̲x—on Gitxsan territory. He discusses the importance of reaching beyond the physical realm and learning from "all worldly beings" in order to become connected to the spiritual. The imagery and poetic reflections on water teach us to dive deeper into teaching and learning that prioritizes the urgency of land and water issues. Hetxw'ms Gyetxw explains how personification is used in traditional Gitxsan multi-sensory storytelling experiences to ensure that "the idea and law that all life is equal and essential to one another for survival is always present in our stories and our society. It's like giving human rights to all things, as the Gitxsan never view humanity as being on top but simply as one part of the world" (page 205). Perhaps this will prompt you to reorganize your worldview, breaking down the hierarchy that so many of us have been taught.

Reanna McKay (Merasty)'s cover art helps to bridge the first book in the Footbridge series, *Resurgence*, with this text. Her imagery of the footbridge depicts the connections between land and water, the journey of individuals on the path to reconciliation, and the blending of Indigenous and Western worldviews. Becoming aware of the connections between land, water, and all living beings is an important aspect of land-based learning that honours the ongoing cyclical processes that are essential to life on Earth.

Together, the contributors encourage us to view the world around us from the perspective of "always being respectful of the reciprocal relationships we are responsible for as human beings" (Henhawk, page 185). Taking this view can help us embrace the changes needed within our own education, or more broadly, as inhabitants of this planet, to become more attuned to the land. We hope these concluding texts inspire you to re-set your priorities and initiate the process of renewing your connection to land and place. We hope you will carry these perspectives in your journey beyond the pages of this text and into your everyday reflections and actions.

CONNECTING ONLINE

Post reflections from your own learning or share how you take up these ideas in your educational setting using the hashtags #FootbridgeRenewalBook and #FootbridgeRenewal.

Start First With a Good Mind

DAN HENHAWK is an Assistant Professor in the Faculty of Kinesiology and Recreation Management at the University of Manitoba. His research interests revolve around Western conceptualizations of leisure and Indigenous ways of knowing and being. He is interested in the tensions between leisure, neo-colonialism, decolonization, and issues of sustainability within recreation and leisure. Dan is Kanien'kehá:ka from the Six Nations of the Grand River.

ALWAYS GO into the garden with a Good Mind. This teaching was given to me during a workshop about traditional Haudenosaunee gardening. While some might see this as simply a call to always have a positive attitude, it is not. The rest of the teaching is that you must go into the garden with a Good Mind because if you don't, the plants that sustain us will feel that negative energy and be adversely affected. This teaching is intimately connected to an Indigenous worldview that human beings live in a reciprocal relationship with those non-human relations that exist in the world. For the Kanien'kehá:ka (Mohawk) people, it is also related to the word *Onkwehonwe*, a term we use to describe ourselves. Onkwehonwe, as it has been explained to me, means "Original People" or "to live originally." This refers to the idea that to live originally, we have responsibilities as human beings—beginning with treating our relations with respect to nurture and sustain them, just as they nurture and sustain us.

This teaching came at a point when I was learning and unlearning my perspectives and attitudes toward my culture, my self-identity, and my relationships to others. I had to unlearn the intrusive colonial perspective that Indigenous cultures are primitive and destined for extinction and have no "real" value in the contemporary moment. I also had to unlearn the popular sentiment that our knowledge was lost. When I lamented to a mentor about the cultural knowledge that was seemingly lost, she replied that it's not that Indigenous knowledges are lost, but rather that human beings have stopped listening. I had to rethink my understanding of Indigenous knowledges and recognize that teachings from our relations are dependent on our willingness to engage with, listen to, and learn from those relations. I also had to learn that such knowledges have a place in the present, as Indigenous Peoples push forward movements of cultural resurgence and decolonization. These teachings fundamentally challenged my anthropocentric understanding of how to exist in the world and forced me to reflect on how one might live in a reciprocal relationship with non-human relations and the land. Learning how to live in the world differently, and with such an Indigenous ethic, is a process that requires continual reflection on oneself and one's engagement with the world.

In my work as a professor, I'm interested in colonialism's relationship to the types of recreation and leisure activities we engage in. I'm also interested in how Indigenous ways of knowing and being impact how we think about leisure, and consequently, the activities we practise. In graduate school, I studied how our understandings of leisure—and by extension, our participation in sport and other recreational activities—were produced by and connected to histories of colonization. For example, there are documented histories of European games and sports being used within the curriculum of Indian residential schools in Canada to indoctrinate Indigenous children into the values and beliefs of settler-colonial society. Within these histories, there are also stories of how participating in such games and sports helped Indigenous children deal with the traumas they were experiencing. Such histories raise many questions, not only about the colonial nature of education and the activities that were used to indoctrinate Indigenous children, but also about our present-day engagement in activities that stem from those histories. We must be aware of the colonial history of these activities, as well as the ways that engaging in them might perpetuate colonialism.

I teach an introductory course on outdoor education and recreation that brings in a critical analysis of the historical and colonial formations of these pursuits. I introduce students to the underpinnings of colonialism, drawing connections to racism and white supremacy, the positioning of Christianity as superior to Indigenous cultures, and the impacts of capitalist ideologies on the land, and ultimately, on Indigenous cultures. It is a constant challenge to get students to think about their relationship to the outdoors and their recreational pursuits, and how engaging in these activities might perpetuate issues of colonialism. I might begin by asking students to think about how their outdoor recreational activities reflect colonial influences. For example, students who have participated in Scouts may not realize the influence of the scouting movement on perpetuating a settler-colonial ideology that views land as a resource and something to be tamed.

I may also challenge students to think more deeply about the connections of these activities to historical formations of capitalism. For example, do their outdoor recreation activities require equipment or clothing that perpetuates a cycle of production and consumption that has a negative impact on the environment?

In any case, the goal is to challenge students to be conscious and aware of how their seemingly simple engagement in outdoor recreational pursuits may contribute to the perpetuation of colonialism, or perhaps offer a way to address oppression and achieve social justice. In the latter regard, much work is being done to address issues of equity, accessibility, and the inclusion of people with varying abilities. From an Indigenous perspective, addressing colonialism may be achieved in our participation in leisure activities that reflect a relationship to the land that offers a way of being that is more in keeping with the idea of starting first with a Good Mind.

It is interesting to ponder how our leisure activities might change if we shifted our mindset to reflect the teaching of starting with a Good Mind. What if, instead of using these activities to satisfy our own individual desires or cope with our own stress, we approached them with an ethic of care for the environment? What would happen if we approached the world, and our own activities, with an understanding of our obligations as human beings to live in respectful relations with each other and with all our relations on the land, in the water, and throughout the cosmos? How might we engage students in physical education, outdoor education, or sport in ways that break the cycle of colonialism, power, and oppression? Perhaps we can begin with the teaching to always start with a Good Mind, from a place of always being respectful of the reciprocal relationships we are responsible for as human beings.

Educator Connections

Read the editors' thoughts and engage in reflection. Respond to the questions that follow on your own or with your colleague(s).

PERSONAL CONNECTIONS

Christine: Dan Henhawk's essay serves as a profound reminder to me to constantly re-evaluate my purpose and path to ensure that I am not overwhelmed by the colonial worldview that the ultimate purpose of life is work, productivity, and the desire for wealth. As someone who loves to take on all the things (including getting multiple university degrees, starting a business, consulting, writing curriculum, and joining sports teams), I need Dan's reminder to slow down and reimagine what leisure could mean if I centred the needs of the Earth and all our relations rather than satisfying my own individual desires or coping with my own stress. I find myself asking: What are my obligations to the land? To water? To other relations?

Katya: The idea of teaching with a good mind and rethinking leisure connects to a message shared by Niigaan Sinclair at a professional learning session in 2022 and in his book, *Wînipêk*. When an eagle's wings get wet, they need time to dry and reactivate the oils in their feathers so they can fly again. He writes: "The oil in its [a feather's] spine keeps its filaments connected. When they are separated, all one has to do is gently stroke the middle spine and distribute the oils so the filaments connect. When eagles experience this, such as when they get wet or in a fight, they will rub against a rock or another eagle, caring for themselves."[1] I recently watched two eagles who appeared to be fighting grasp talons above a lake. One pushed the other down toward the water, close enough to get its wings wet. I witnessed this beautiful, wet eagle perch several metres from me as it waited for its wings to dry. Had I not heard Niigaan Sinclair speak about this, I would have wondered why the eagle was just sitting there leisurely. But this time had a purpose: it was working to restore

---

1   *Wînipêk: Visions of Canada from an Indigenous Centre*, by Niigaan Sinclair (McClelland & Stewart, 2024), 275.

186

itself and taking important time to do what its body, mind, and feathers needed. I see a connection between Dan Henhawk's and Niigaan Sinclair's words, and both have helped me to rethink leisure more relationally.

EDUCATOR INQUIRY AND ACTIONS

- What do you think your obligations are to the land? To water? To other relations?

- How has this essay shifted your perspective of leisure?

- What are some ways in which "seemingly simple engagement in outdoor recreational pursuits may contribute to the perpetuation of colonialism"? What are some ways these pursuits might "offer a way to address oppression and achieve social justice"?

- As more teachers recognize the benefits and value of being and learning outside and venture into land-based learning, how do you think land-based learning should be viewed in relation to the terms *recreation* and *leisure*?

- Discuss some obstacles to teaching and learning with a Good Mind that you have faced in and outside the classroom.

- Do you ever stop to think about why you do what you do? Reflect on this in relation to your own teaching. Consider some of the activities you did yesterday in your classroom with students and think critically about why you did what you did.

- The UN Convention on the Rights of the Child states that children have the right to play and the right to rest.[2] Think about the choices that students have access to in your school community. Do they have opportunities to choose from a variety of engaging activities and to rest when needed?

- As a school team, list some of your responsibilities and obligations to the land and to each other. Display this list prominently and come back to it often.

---

2   United Nations, Convention on the Rights of the Child (November 20, 1989), ohchr.org/en/instruments
    -mechanisms/instruments/convention-rights-child.

Classroom Connections

Introduce to students the narrative and the Connected Concepts you wish to focus on. Use the following questions, prompts, and resource suggestions to guide student learning.

CONNECTED CONCEPTS

- Reimagining leisure
- Indigenous ways of doing/being
- Learning/unlearning
- Sustainability

CONNECTING TO SELF: PROMPTS FOR PERSONAL REFLECTION

❭ Beginning

- How does your attitude at the outset of an activity affect the outcome?

- What obligations or responsibilities do you currently have?

❭ Bridging

- What do you do to take care of and live in harmony with the land? With water? With other relations?

- What more can you do to take care of the land? Of water? Of other relations?

● Beyond

- How do you define "leisure"?

- What connections do you see between leisure and privilege?

- How do the outdoor recreational activities you participate in reflect colonial influences? Think about aspects such as location, uniforms, rules, and equipment.

CONNECTING TO COMMUNITY: PROMPTS FOR LEARNING CIRCLES

Beginning

- Share your favourite leisure activities and why they are important to you.

- Discuss your understandings of the terms *leisure*, *sport*, and *recreation*.

Bridging

- Share a ritual you do to cleanse your mind.

- Describe how you feel when participating in your favourite leisure activity and how this might be helpful to you in various ways.

Beyond

- Drawing on Dan Henhawk's idea of "learning how to live in the world differently," reflect on what you might need to learn or unlearn as you engage with the world.

- Discuss some obstacles to approaching the world with a Good Mind that you have faced.

CONNECTING TO LAND-BASED LEARNING

Beginning

- Choose something you do on the land that you can approach with a Good Mind. Make this part of your routine for a specific period of time.

- Try out a variety of activities that connect to land within a chosen time frame. Which activities drained your energy and which activities gave you energy?

Bridging

- Look at brochures aimed at tourists and think about how land-based leisure is advertised to sell the idea of a place.

- Ritual and ceremony can be used to create a good mindset. Learn about a new ritual, ceremony, or practice.

● Beyond

- Interview an Elder to find out how they spend their time during an average day. Compare and contrast this with your routines and priorities. What changes would you like to make? You could also try this with a child to see if you gain inspiration from their routine.

- Research the history of your favourite sport. How has colonization, specifically connected to displacement from land, impacted that sport? Or how has the sport impacted the land?

CONNECTING TO LAND BACK

- Dan Henhawk's essay explores a key tension between colonial values and the purpose of life according to Kanien'kehá:ka tradition. Explore the differences and similarities between Western sports and activities and traditional Indigenous games and activities, such as lacrosse or hunting. How do the ways people participate in these activities showcase differences in worldview and cultural values? Look specifically at the concept of Minopimatisiwin (the Good Life) and compare it with current capitalist/neo-liberal/colonial perspectives of success. With Land Back comes the freedom to enact Indigenous conceptualizations of time and to reimagine leisure from a community-based perspective. How would you spend your time if you didn't have to worry about colonial perspectives of productivity?

CONNECTIONS TO OTHER INDIGENOUS RESOURCES

Books

When We Are Kind, by Monique Gray Smith (Orca Book Publishers, 2020; ages 3–5).

Using simple text and illustrations that are affirming of Indigenous cultures, this picture book asks readers to think about what kindness means to them, making connections to wellness, leisure, and self-care. Available in English, French, and dual-language Diné and English.

Kihcite Metawewina: Playing With a Great Heart, by Blair Robillard (Manitoba Aboriginal Sports and Recreation Council, 2020).
This book provides examples of traditional Indigenous games from different nations, along with instructions on how to play them.

The Seven Circles: Indigenous Teachings for Living Well, by Chelsey Luger and Thosh Collins (HarperOne, 2022).
This self-help guide by Indigenous well-being experts offers practical ways to achieve mental, spiritual, emotional, and physical health.

Film

First Arctic Winter Games, directed by Dennis Sawyer and R. C. Gibson (National Film Board of Canada, 1970). <www.nfb.ca/film/first-arctic-winter-games/>.
This short documentary is about the first Arctic Winter Games, held in Yellowknife, Northwest Territories, in 1970.

The Grizzlies, directed by Miranda de Pencier (Mongrel Media, 2018).
This film is based on the true story of a youth lacrosse team established to help combat an outbreak of youth suicide in the community of Kugluktuk, Nunavut.

Indian Horse, directed by Stephen Campanelli (Elevation Pictures, 2017).
This adaptation of Ojibwe writer Richard Wagamese's award-winning novel sheds light on the dark history of Canada's Indian residential schools, with a focus on hockey.

Keepers of the Game, directed by Judd Ehrlich (Tribeca Digital Studios, 2016).
In this documentary, members of an Indigenous girls' lacrosse team try to prove the game is their rightful inheritance.

Stories From Our Land, Vol. 2: Strength, Flexibility, and Endurance, directed by Allen Auksaq (National Film Board of Canada, 2013). <collection.nfb.ca/film/stories-from-our-land-vol2-strength-iu>.
Two athletes demonstrate Inuit games of strength, flexibility, and endurance and share their perspectives on how traditional games were more than just leisure activities, supporting important life lessons for healthy muscles and minds.

Online

Traditional Inuit Games. <www.athropolis.com/news-upload/11-data/index.htm>.

This website was created by grade 6 students at Aqsarniit School in Iqaluit, Nunavut, to share their learning on how to play traditional Inuit games. The instructions use kid-friendly language and step-by-step photographs.

Podcast

Metawewin, hosted by Elijah Buffalo. <podcasters.spotify.com/pod/show/elijah-buffalo>.

This podcast shares an Indigenous athlete's perspectives of sports, health, and fitness and makes connections between sports and systemic racism. The podcast explores the importance of maintaining a healthy balance in life and the relationship Indigenous people have with sport.

Mah! (Listen!)

RÉAL CARRIÈRE is Nehinuw (Swampy Cree) and Métis from Cumberland House, Saskatchewan. He was home-schooled and grew up on the land, with no road access, running water, or electricity. His current research focuses on Nehinuwak political theories, Indigenous methodology, and Indigenous political representation. He is an Assistant Professor at the University of Manitoba in Political Studies, with a specific focus on Indigenous politics. He is passionate about canoeing, storytelling, Indigenous knowledge, and social justice.

———

I HAVE BEEN INSPIRED BY the resurgence of land-based education in recent years. In my home community, I have seen how young learners are provided with learning experiences outside of the classroom. These experiences are much more common now than when I was a student only a decade ago. However, I am concerned that the increased popularity of "land-based education" has created a rush toward implementation without deeper understanding. Deeper understanding takes time and effort. We must begin by reflecting on our position in relation to land-based education and then critically assess what land-based education is. If we do not make this effort, land-based education will not live up to its potential as a transformative and Indigenous method of education. I hope that by the end of this essay you will understand why it is so important to re-envision the idea of land-based education.

I want to begin by discussing my positionality in relation to land-based education. *Positionality* is a process used in Indigenous academic circles that identifies one's connection truthfully. How do you know that I know anything about land-based education? Land-based education has always been close to my heart. I grew up on the land in the Traditional Territory of my Nehinuwak ancestors, 50 kilometres from the nearest neighbour. While I completed the standard Canadian educational system, I also spent significant time learning the ways of the Nehinuwak/Ininiwak people. Hunting, trapping, fishing, canoeing, making fire, fetching water—the land-based tasks of my ancestors—were an integral part of my education. Land-based education is not a metaphor or something abstract. Despite my connection to it, I still do not feel worthy of being considered a "land-based" expert.

Now that I have shared my connection to land-based education, I want to engage with my view of "land-based" through the Cree concept of "Mah." "Mah" is something I heard a lot when I was out on the land. "Mah" is a Nehinuw expression used to get someone's attention.

It can be a question: *Mah? Listen?*

It can also be a command: *MAH! LISTEN!*

In either case, when someone says "Mah," you must stop what you are doing and listen. You would only say "Mah" to draw someone's attention to something that needs to be heard. You cannot keep doing what you are doing if you intend to listen well. I have titled this paper "Mah! (Listen!)" because I want you to take time to listen. Listen to my words and to what is in your heart. If you want to understand what land-based education is, you must take time to stop and reflect on what you are trying to do with your land-based education.

Mah!

Land-based education is not just about land. The "land" of "land-based" is a metaphor for the space that Indigenous people exist in when we are truly being Indigenous. Since we do not solely exist on the land, in this case "land" also includes spaces inhabited by water and air. Thus, the "land" both is and is not a specific place. This point is important, because while it is critical for Indigenous Peoples to understand their own land, the "land" of "land-based" is not limited to one's own land. I have learned many things outside of my own territory. Furthermore, the "land" of "land-based" is more than a place. The land is spiritual. The land is physical. Thus, the land is a place of diverse learning. It is a place of experiential learning. It is a place of abstract reflection. It is a place of collective and individual knowledge.

Having a single concept of "land-based education" is great for creating a common language and frame of reference, but "land-based" can mean a lot of different things to different people. Thus, I do not think we should be defining what it is. The issue with any such definition is that it limits our understanding to a specific place or practice. Practices of "land-based" education have become spectacles for social media. A photo of people standing next to a butchered moose is not land-based education. Land-based education happens in the space and moments before and after that photo. Land-based experiences should be shared, but never at the expense of another living creature.

MAH!

You cannot understand land if you do not listen. If you do not take the time to listen with an open heart, you will never understand land-based education, because the true journey of land-based education happens in your mind, heart, and soul. Land-based education is the living practice of Indigenous philosophies and worldviews. These practices differ from person to person and nation to nation. We must reflect on our own situation before we take a step farther down the path of land-based education. Even an expert in land-based education has to constantly reflect on their own practices. I know that my personal role models, whom I consider to be experts of land-based education, continue to do so.

Land-based education is important to me because only when I am on the land do I truly feel Indigenous. This happens when I go paddling. I live in Winnipeg, and I paddle a lot up and down the Red and Assiniboine Rivers. This is not my home territory. Yet when I truly get in the zone of land-based education, despite any urban distractions, I can feel the connection to my ancestors with every stroke of the paddle. In my mind's eye, I visualize my ancestors passing through this territory, because some of my ancestors did travel through Winnipeg. I visualize going with my mother and father down my home river. At times, I feel like I can see back in time thousands of years to some ancient ancestor. At other times, I can see into the future, as my children and their children pass through the land. I try to teach my children about the importance of the land so that I may one day connect with them far into the future as they think about me.

Land-based education is important because it is a pathway to think about the past, present, and future. Only when I am engaged in land-based learning do I truly feel Indigenous.

Mah!

Ekosi.

Educator Connections

Read the editors' thoughts and engage in reflection. Respond to the questions that follow on your own or with your colleague(s).

PERSONAL CONNECTIONS

Christine: Réal Carrière's essay offers foundational knowledge for educators who want to begin their journey of embracing Indigenous theories of land-based education. To be honest, when the idea for a textbook around the theme of "land-based education" was introduced, I was simultaneously worried and excited. I was worried because as an Indigenous person growing up in the city, and with limited outdoor experience, I knew this was an area where I struggled. At the same time, I was excited because I knew I would have the opportunity to learn from some incredible teachers. I'm thankful Réal has offered this essay, and I'll refer to it as a guide on this journey. His advice to just "listen" is a concrete example of how educators like me can venture into land-based experiences with open minds and hearts.

Katya: So much discussion in education focuses on perceived "destinations" in terms of prescribed outcomes or achievement standards. Réal Carrière's essay reminds me that land-based learning is not a destination, or a metaphor, or an abstract idea. The concept of "Mah" feels like a wake-up call to listen thoughtfully to the web of possibilities and understandings that come from the concept of "land-based." I think there are facets of the education system that will have trouble with this definition because of its flexibility, but I see that as beautiful and necessary. Too often we want things to be measurable, static, predictable, and unpackable, and then repackable. As someone who is not Indigenous, I have a relationship with land that can never be fully aligned with Indigenous ways of knowing. I strive to approach learning from land and nature with an open heart, and feel that these ways of being and understanding are helping me become a more aware teacher, mother, and human on this Earth. In this time of climate emergency, I think the Earth is speaking loudly, and I want to find ways to listen and respond.

EDUCATOR INQUIRY AND ACTIONS

- What is your positionality in relation to the topic of land-based education? Consider your worldviews and share your specific cultural perspectives.

- When did you first hear the term *land-based*? What were your initial thoughts, feelings, and questions about this term?

- Why do you think there has been a resurgence of land-based education? Discuss your school's approach to land-based curricular connections. Have there been important shifts in these in recent years?

- Has Réal Carrière's essay deepened your understanding of land-based education? If so, how?

- Create a visual continuum to show where you are currently situated in relation to integrating land-based education in your teaching practice and to set goals for where you want to be.

- In what ways have you engaged in land-based education with your heart? With your mind? With your spirit?

- Réal Carrière describes spending time learning land-based tasks. Take a mini audit of the types of tasks you ask students to complete each day. How many of them are transferable to other settings? How many support learning on the land?

- Reread Réal Carrière's essay with your school team. Invite readers to say "Mah!" out loud anytime they have a comment or question to share. Continue reading when they are done sharing so that you do not lose the rhythm of the piece but have inserted your perspectives alongside Carrière's.

- Réal Carrière describes his experiences of hunting, canoeing, fishing, trapping, making fire, and fetching water as an integral rather than separate part of his education. What is currently viewed by others as being on the periphery of your education that you know is integral?

- Does the idea of "Mah" change or challenge your idea of land-based education? If so, describe how.

Classroom Connections

Introduce to students the narrative and the Connected Concepts you wish to focus on. Use the following questions, prompts, and resource suggestions to guide student learning.

CONNECTED CONCEPTS

- Identity
- Ancestral homelands
- Worldview

CONNECTING TO SELF: PROMPTS FOR PERSONAL REFLECTION

) **Beginning**

- Write down words or draw images that come to mind when you think of the land.

- Describe your connection to the land.

- What have you learned about Canada's history in relation to Indigenous Peoples' rights to land? Who have you learned from?

- What do you want to know about land-based learning?

● **Beyond**

- Consider the Cree concept of "Mah" ("listen"). How can you incorporate active listening into your own life?

- What does the author mean when he says, "Land-based education is not just about land"? Reflect on the broader implications of land-based education beyond physical spaces.

CONNECTING TO COMMUNITY: PROMPTS FOR LEARNING CIRCLES

▶ **Beginning**

- Describe the place where you live (home/neighbourhood/city). After listening to others' descriptions, think about how they are similar or different.

- Share an experience when you learned on the land.

▶ **Bridging**

- Describe a place or practice that connects you to your ancestors.

- Réal Carrière shares why land-based education is important to him. Share your personal thoughts and feelings about the importance of land-based education.

● **Beyond**

- Describe your personal philosophy or worldview and how you live out or practise this. If there's something about this you want to continue or change, share that as well.

- Réal Carrière states, "I do not think we should be defining what [land-based education] is." Reflect on this statement.

CONNECTING TO LAND-BASED LEARNING

) Beginning

- Find a sit spot outside and listen to the land. What do you hear?

- Go outdoors and look for one mammal, one insect, one bird, and one home. Try thinking about the environment from their perspective.

) Bridging

- Scroll through social media and look for hashtags such as #land and #landbased. Take time to debate and decide if the photos and captions you find align with Réal Carrière's view of what *land-based* means.

- Attend an Indigenous event in your local area, such as an Orange Shirt Day or National Indigenous Peoples Day event, or an Indigenous-led bike or walking tour with a decolonizing focus.

● Beyond

- Write a one-sentence definition of the term *land-based*. Come back to it after taking a walk. Come back to it after learning from an Elder. Come back to it often and revise it. See how it changes and how you are changed too.

- Plan to go for a paddle. Think about all you need to do to prepare. Then reflect on what you have learned from the planning process alone.

- Attend an Indigenous ceremony in your area. What new understandings of land and land-based education do you have after doing so?

CONNECTING TO LAND BACK

- This essay addresses the key tension that arises for many Indigenous people living outside their territory or homeland. Acts such as paddling, as shared by Réal Carrière, are a way of connecting to land-based practices. This essay reminds us that Land Back connections can be made not only through actions such as returning to the land and traditional practices, but also by reconnecting to Indigenous ways of knowing (listening). The Cree concept of "Mah" draws "attention to something that needs to be heard." How have Western notions of teaching and learning affected our ability to listen to and learn from the land?

CONNECTING TO OTHER INDIGENOUS RESOURCES

Books

The Birchbark House, by Louise Erdrich (Hyperion, 2002; ages 8–12).
This middle-grade novel highlights the daily life of a historical Indigenous community. It focuses on a seven-year-old girl who lives with an adopted family after a smallpox epidemic kills her family.

Restoring the Kinship Worldview: Indigenous Voices Introduce 28 Precepts for Rebalancing Life on Planet Earth, by Wahinkpe Topa (Four Arrows) and Darcia Narvaez (North Atlantic Books, 2022).
This book provides passages excerpted from speeches of Indigenous leaders that honour the Earth and the greater good, with a focus on moving toward a more egalitarian and sustainable future.

Online

"Lands & Natural Resources Proclamation Law Video 2016," Opaskwayak.
<www.youtube.com/watch?v=tiTOOKfnQpk>.
Opaskwayak Cree Nation is described as the "First-First Nation to Proclaim Environmental Laws." This video includes testimonials from leaders on the importance of environmental laws and protection of land and water.

Podcasts

"Indigenous Public Art Tour Through Winnipeg," *Unreserved*, hosted by Rosanna Deerchild, CBC Radio, October 15, 2021.
<www.cbc.ca/radio/unreserved/unreserved-tour-explores-winnipeg-s -history-from-indigenous-public-art-lens-1.6200508>.
This episode focuses on Winnipeg's history through the contributions of Indigenous art in public spaces.

"Dr. Shawn Wilson: Strengthening Relations with Indigenous Knowledge," Melbourne Poche Centre for Indigenous Health.
<soundcloud.com/unimelbpoche/dr-shawn-wilson-strengthening -relations-with-indigenous-knowledge>.
Drawing on his seminal book *Research Is Ceremony*, Dr. Wilson discusses Indigenous research methodology and how we can use protocols and ceremony to strengthen our relationships with knowledge.

The Art of Learning and Storytelling: "A Gitxsan Ode to Water"

HETXW'MS GYETXW, also known as Brett D. Huson (he/him/his), is from the Gitxsan Nation of the Northwest Interior of British Columbia. Growing up in this strong matrilineal society, Brett developed a passion for the culture, land, and politics of his people, and a desire to share their knowledge and stories. Brett is the founder and president of Aluu'taa, an Indigenous knowledges research hub. His award-winning Mothers of Xsan series for middle-grade readers is part of a larger vision to share the worlds of the Gitxsan Nation.

––––––––––

A Gitxsan Ode to Water

In the Gitxsan realm, where mountains touch sky,
Water's sacredness, like a lullaby.
A gentle current, a mother's embrace,
Nourishing the land with abundant grace.

Like a shimmer that reflects life's tale,
Water's sacred whispers never fail.
A song of healing, a symphony of dreams,
Awakening the spirit as it gracefully streams.

Water, the lifeblood, an eternal flow,
Connecting all beings, high and low.
A thread that weaves through time and space,
A reminder of our shared human embrace.

In every drop, a story unfolds,
Of unity, resilience, and truths untold.
Water, the healer, washing away strife,
Offering solace, the elixir of life.

Oh, let us honour this precious gift,
Through actions kind, let our spirits lift.
For in Gitxsan wisdom, we can see,
The sacredness of water, forever free.

By Hetxw'ms Gyetxw (Brett D. Huson)

A Gitxsan Ode to Water

In the Gitxsan realm, where mountains touch sky,
Water's sacredness, like a lullaby.
A gentle current, a mother's embrace,
Nourishing the land with abundant grace.

Like a shimmer that reflects life's tale,
Water's sacred whispers never fail.
A song of healing, a symphony of dreams,
Awakening the spirit as it gracefully streams.

Water, the lifeblood, an eternal flow,
Connecting all beings, high and low.
A thread that weaves through time and space,
A reminder of our shared human embrace.

In every drop, a story unfolds,
Of unity, resilience, and truths untold.
Water, the healer, washing away strife,
Offering solace, the elixir of life.

Oh, let us honour this precious gift,
Through actions kind, let our spirits lift.
For in Gitxsan wisdom, we can see,
The sacredness of water, forever free.

The Pacific Northwest of what settlers now call British Columbia has a storied past that expands far beyond the last two glacial maximums. The stories that have survived since time immemorial were not simply forms of entertainment and social therapy, but also methods of sharing knowledge and disseminating ideas.

To the Gitxsan people, yuhlimx is the word used to describe our education process. In English, the Gitxsan people describe yuhlimx as "words of wisdom." This process begins with your aunts and uncles in your house group or family unit. Yuhlimx, most importantly, happens through storytelling.

The way of life on the coast depended on communicating ideas, and exploring emergent methods of existence in a way all thinkers could relate to was important. In complex societies, you'll never agree on everything, so sharing knowledge and new information through storytelling is crucial to the coastal peoples. The Gitxsan often share knowledge and ways of being through music, poetry, performance, dance, and fine arts. In "A Gitxsan Ode to Water," there is an expression of the important role water plays in everyday life. The personification of grandmother water brings an element of human rights to water. The spiritual realm teaches us that all life exists as one energy.

Personification of all worldly beings was often present in Gitxsan storytelling. Western anthropology hypothesized that this indicated a belief in deities and gods. However, the leaders and teachers used personification to ensure that the idea and law that all forms of life are equal and essential to one another for survival is always present in our stories and our society. It's like giving human rights to all things, as the Gitxsan never view humanity as being on top but simply as one part of the world.

The coastal people have always believed that memory is closely related to all the senses, not just to sight. So, as we move through life, yuhlimx̲ is always accompanied by different aspects of memory, such as a smudge, to remind us of a clear mind, love, and good intent. Being on the land engages all the senses, and as we smell the scents and hear the sounds of the lessons we receive, we often remember what we are learning. Our senses help us retain information; this is even more important in oral traditions, where collective knowledge is often shared in immense gatherings to ensure consensus on guiding knowledge.

Educator Connections

Read the editors' thoughts and engage in reflection. Respond to the questions that follow on your own or with your colleague(s).

PERSONAL CONNECTIONS

Christine: I had to read Hetxw'ms Gyetxw's poem out loud to truly appreciate the rhythmic flow and rich metaphors highlighting the interconnectedness of water and all beings on Earth. I found myself reciting the poem with a wave-like cadence, evoking the life-giving essence of water, with my voice pushing forward and then retreating again like waves on the shore. I'm excited to use this poem in my classroom to get students thinking about Indigenous knowledge, environmental stewardship, and gratitude for the water.

Katya: The notion that "In every drop, a story unfolds" is sticking with me. As I learn more about water issues, the dislocation of communities away from water, and how many families live for generations with unclean water in Canada, my understandings of the effects of colonialism deepen. I want to do more to uphold a reverence for the sacredness of water in my daily life and in my teaching. I think sometimes I take water for granted. These turbulent water stories are calmed by poems like this one, which reminds me about the healing and purifying qualities of water. What if honouring the "precious gift" of water was a curricular outcome?

EDUCATOR INQUIRY AND ACTIONS

- How does this poem illustrate cultural and land-based teachings?

- Using the poetic frame, rhythm, and pattern that Hetxw'ms Gyetxw provides, have each member of your school team draft one stanza to add to "A Gitxsan Ode to Water" that reflects their personal connections to water. Reread the poem and then take turns sharing your individual stanzas to create an extended multi-voiced poem.

- Consider the differences between patrilineal and matrilineal societies.

- Analyze the imagery in relation to the poem. How does the imagery enhance the themes of the poem?

- Think about one of your go-to classroom routines. How might you rethink this routine to make it a more engaging and multisensory experience?

- What are ways that your school community uses or misuses water? Think about daily teaching practices and find ways to tweak them to honour the sacredness of water.

- How can you find space for connections to water within existing curriculum across disciplines?

Classroom Connections

Introduce to students the poem, artwork, and narrative and the Connected Concepts you wish to focus on. Use the following questions, prompts, and resource suggestions to guide student learning.

CONNECTED CONCEPTS

- Sacredness
- Storytelling
- Matrilineal society
- Water as lifeblood

CONNECTING TO SELF: PROMPTS FOR PERSONAL REFLECTION

) Beginning

- What does this poem make you think about? How does it make you feel?

- Recite the poem out loud. What do you notice?

) Bridging

- Does this poem remind you of any experiences in your own life?

- How do you connect to the sacredness of water?

● **Beyond**

- What yuhlimx (or words of wisdom) have guided you?

- Consider the role of water in supporting life, from the earliest stages in the womb to the growth of plants and the survival of animals. How does this interconnectedness emphasize the vital importance of water in our world?

CONNECTING TO COMMUNITY: PROMPTS FOR LEARNING CIRCLES

❱ **Beginning**

- View and discuss the imagery of Hetxw'ms Gyetxw's art alongside Sonny Assu's work. Share what you notice or wonder, particularly about the geography portrayed in the images.

- Share which line of the poem resonated with you the most and explain why.

- Share your observations of this poem and the accompanying artwork.

❱ **Bridging**

- Discuss how the poetic rhythm relates to water.

- Share how the imagery tells us a story about where Hetxw'ms Gyetxw is from and how you know this.

- Reflect on if, how, or why protecting and defending water is different or more difficult than protecting land.

● **Beyond**

- Share a story, memory, or adventure that involves being connected to water. Consider how your senses have helped you remember and share this.

- Explain one way water can be used for healing.

- Share a story from your own or another culture and describe the lesson or value it teaches.

CONNECTING TO LAND-BASED LEARNING

) Beginning

- Write your own ode to water or to your mother.

- Grab a cup of water. Express to the water your gratitude and appreciation for all that it provides to life on Earth. Reflect on how it felt to express your gratitude. If possible, use the water you praised to water a plant and support a new cycle of growth.

- Locate Gitxsan territory on a map. Research to find the agreements made on the land; for example, is it ceded or unceded territory or involved in a treaty?

) Bridging

- Who are the water walkers? How can you support them?

- Look at the artwork and compare and contrast it to the traditional artwork of other West Coast nations. How has the natural environment influenced the imagery?

● Beyond

- Connect "A Gitxsan Ode to Water" to Tyna Legault Taylor's essay "Homelands and Waterways" (page 75) and Peatr Thomas's art and writing in "Miskwaadesi Maada Ookii Gikendamowin/Turtle Sharing Knowledge (From the Sturgeon)" (page 65). They represent three Indigenous perspectives of water. What new understandings come from connecting their work and viewpoints of water?

- Connect with an Elder to learn more about water teachings or local water ceremonies.

CONNECTING TO LAND BACK

- Many Indigenous territories in British Columbia are unceded through treaties or land agreements, which has led to land-rights disputes between Indigenous communities and the government. Look up the historic *Delgamuukw v. British Columbia* (1997) Supreme Court Case involving Hetxw'ms Gyetxw's home territory of the Gitxsan, which proved land rights and oral testimony as legitimate.[1] This court case helps to demonstrate the tension between the government and the Land Back movement. According to land defender Kolin Sutherland-Wilson, blockading and defending land from settler colonial resource extraction and disruption, including logging, pipelines, and railways, has become part of "Gitxsan tradition" due to "the rail line across Gitxsan territory [that] has been blockaded for more than a hundred years."[2] Research this territorial land dispute or another one closer to your home. How do the courts affirm Indigenous rights to land?

CONNECTIONS TO OTHER INDIGENOUS RESOURCES

Books

Just Like Grandma, by Kim Rogers (Heartdrum, 2023; ages 4–8).
This picture book supports the theme of role models and learning from Elders as it shares Wichita heritage/Native American perspectives and connections to beading and dancing.

Missing Nimâmâ, by Melanie Florence (Clockwise Press, 2015; ages 8–12). This fictional story weaves together the voice of a young girl and the spirit of her mother to address the realities of systemic, gender-based violence and the crisis of missing and murdered Indigenous women and girls.

Animals of the Salish Sea, by Melaney Gleeson-Lyall (Native Northwest, 2016; ages 9–11).
This book shares animals and teachings connected to the Coast Salish marine environment through the distinctive art of 13 Coast Salish artists.

---

1 For more information, see Gérald A. Beaudoin, "Delgamuukw Case," The Canadian Encyclopedia, August 18, 2017, www.thecanadianencyclopedia.ca/en/article/delgamuukw-case; "Episode 1: The Eviction," *Land Back*, November 15, 2022, www.cbc.ca/listen/cbc-podcasts/1341-landback.

2 Angela Sterritt, "25 Years After the Delgamuukw Case, the Fight for Land Is More Contentious Than Ever," CBC News, November 15, 2022, www.cbc.ca/news/canada/british-columbia/delgamuukw-25-years-later-1.6646687.

Mothers of Xsan series, by Hetxw'ms Gyetxw (Brett D. Huson) (HighWater Press, 2017–present; ages 9–12).
Each book in this series provides informational elements alongside a story following the life cycle of a different female animal of importance to the Gitxsan People, including the sockeye salmon, grizzly bear, and raven.

Online

"Indigenous Knowledges," The Gitxsan. <thegitxsan.ca/>.
Hetxw'ms Gyetxw's (Brett Huson's) website provides information about storytelling, Gitxsan perspectives, resources, connections to art, and climate action.

"The Historic Delgamuukw Land Claims Case: 25 Years Later," CBC Vancouver, November 16, 2022. <www.youtube.com/watch?v=bKqostqKK8g>.
This video provides a brief synopsis of the historic *Delgamuukw* case and how the declaration of Gitxsan and Wet'suwet'en relationship to lands was taken to the Supreme Court of Canada.

Podcast

"Episode 1: The Eviction," *Land Back*, hosted by Angela Sterritt, Episode 1.
<www.cbc.ca/listen/cbc-podcasts/1341-landback/episode/15948638-e1
-the-eviction >.
This episode features a conversation about a territorial dispute that surfaced in 1993 and connects to the historic *Delgamuukw* land claim case, encouraging listeners to think about what the term *land back* might mean to Gitxsan.

Land Connection for Resurgence and Renewal

REANNA MCKAY (MERASTY) is a Nîhithaw artist, writer, and educator from Barren Lands First Nation. Primarily based in Winnipeg, Manitoba, Reanna works in the field of architecture. Inspired by her upbringing in northern Manitoba, she has dedicated her career to amplifying Indigenous voices and advocating for land-based processes.

—————

As a nîhithaw iskwêw (Woodlands Cree woman) artist and architectural intern, the land and water are a source of guidance, influence, and inspiration. I was raised in Barren Lands First Nation, on and along the shores of Reindeer Lake, where I developed a profound reverence for the land and water. The land is where I picked berries with my grandparents and where we hunted moose and built our cabins. The water is where I fished and travelled to and from my community by boat. Experiences with land and water are unique to each Indigenous person as they honour this connection in their own way.

Land and water serve as the theme for *Renewal*, volume 2 of the Footbridge series, and as inspiration for its cover art. The process of creating this cover art began with volume 1 of the series, *Resurgence*. When I created the cover art for *Resurgence*, I took inspiration from the image of a traditional footbridge and the concept of the braid. The footbridge symbolizes the connection between two pieces of land: one that represents Indigenous worldviews and

Resurgence
Digital Image
(Image courtesy of Reanna McKay (Merasty)).

Renewal
Digital Image
(Image courtesy of Reanna McKay (Merasty)).

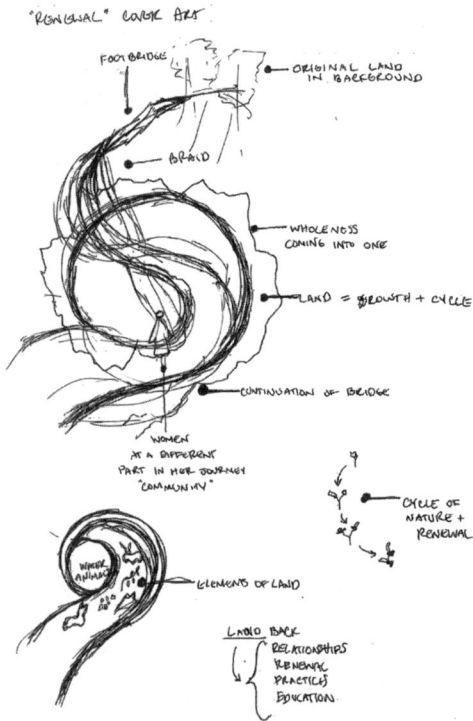

the other a Western classroom. In addition, the footbridge references both the journey of getting over an obstacle and the importance of balance. The end of the footbridge transitions into a braid, which symbolizes the intertwining of knowledge. Each strand of the braid references the different paths we are on as Indigenous people, and our ability to support one another on our journeys.

To create the cover art for *Renewal*, I began by referencing the cover of *Resurgence*, particularly how the intertwining of knowledge comes together to form a path. Within this path are various elements that inhabit the land, including animals and plants, which influence our everyday lives as Indigenous people. For myself, my experience with the land directly influences my work in architecture, through the use of land-based materials and Indigenous knowledge in sustainability. The path creates a circle, symbolizing wholeness and the act of coming together. Encompassed by the path is the element of water and those that live within it. The water is juxtaposed by fire that surrounds and contrasts it.

Travelling along the path is the individual also seen in the *Resurgence* art. She is now at a different part of her journey of reclamation, and ultimately, renewal. She is an educator who is focused on the renewal of Indigenous ways of being in education and of ecological and wholistic balance.

The cover art for volumes 1 and 2 of the Footbridge series started with the story of the traditional footbridge and connection to land. It was created through hand-drawn sketches and digital tools. The art takes inspiration from our inherent connection to culture, community, land, and water as Indigenous Peoples, which is referenced in the use of natural colours and textures. Overall, these works illustrate the role of an educator and the passing of Indigenous knowledge to the next generation.

Educator Connections

Read the editors' thoughts and engage in reflection. Respond to the questions that follow on your own or with your colleague(s).

PERSONAL CONNECTIONS

Christine: The first time I read Reanna McKay (Merasty)'s work was when she submitted her essay on Indigenizing spaces for *Resurgence*.[1] I remember being inspired by that piece, as it shifted my thinking about the ways human-made structures can disrupt or integrate with the natural environment. Then, came her cover art for *Resurgence*—I loved the way she understood the intention for the book to inspire in readers both literal and metaphorical journeys into different ways of thinking and expressing. Now, with the cover of *Renewal*, Reanna has done it again! The way she can take an idea—in this case, highlighting a renewed relationship with land and water—and create such a stunning visual representation is admirable. When I look at the cover, I see a symbiotic relationship where the water, land, and beings coexist and contribute to the Earth's balance.

Katya: I love reading about Reanna McKay (Merasty)'s artistic processes and how her reverence for land and water emerged through experiences with family. I think the symbolism in her artwork gives a pulse to the meaning of the terms *resurgence* and *renewal*. I come back to the cover image of *Resurgence* often; I think it helps guide the work Christine and I are doing together. It highlights the precarious nature of the footbridge and how journeying across a divide may be difficult. The footbridge and braid image strengthens the idea that of artistic expressions and perspectives coming together—in *Resurgence* and *Renewal* and also between nations and knowledge systems. The *Resurgence* cover art makes me wonder if I am on the right track and prompts me to

---

[1] Reanna Merasty, "Indigenizing Spaces: Identity in the Built Environment," in *Resurgence: Engaging With Indigenous Narratives and Cultural Expressions In and Beyond the Classroom,* ed. Christine M'Lot and Katya Adamov-Ferguson (Portage & Main Press, 2022), 145–57.

consider how I can be supportive. The *Renewal* cover image reminds me how we as humans are only one piece of a much larger ecosystem and to hold reverence for all living beings. Indigenous communities and relational approaches remind me of the need to keep this balance of relationships for the sake of the planet.

EDUCATOR INQUIRY AND ACTIONS

- Reanna McKay (Merasty) says, "Experiences with land and water are unique to each Indigenous person as they honour this connection in their own way." What is your experience with land and water and how do you honour this connection?

- Draw or sketch your own land and water connection map, creating a visual representation of personally meaningful landscapes and/or bodies of water. Reflect on how these places have influenced your perspectives, teaching philosophies, and well-being.

- In what ways do you intertwine Indigenous worldviews with Western views in the classroom? How would you visually represent the blending of Indigenous knowledges with Western knowledge?

- Facilitate a story-sharing circle with fellow educators. Have each person share a brief story of a time when they felt connected to nature or learned something from the environment. Consider how storytelling activities like this can be used as a pedagogical tool in the classroom.

- The photo of Reanna McKay (Merasty) when she was a young girl on the land with her dad (on page 212) speaks to the experiences that helped her develop "a profound reverence for the land and water." Consider sharing photos connected to your own learning from the land or to a journey you've taken.

- Consider your own teaching practice. What educational philosophies or practices do you weave in your classroom?

- Where are you in your journey of integrating Indigenous knowledges into your learning spaces?

Classroom Connections

CONNECTING TO SELF: PROMPTS FOR PERSONAL REFLECTION

❯ Beginning

- Look at the cover art for both *Resurgence* and *Renewal*. What do you notice? What stands out to you?

- What are some traditions or customs in your home or community? Think of special foods, holidays, or activities that are important to you.

❯ Bridging

- Compare the cover art for *Resurgence* and *Renewal*. What similarities and differences do you notice?

- Think about the various traditions, values, and ways of doing things you've experienced at home and school and with your friends. How have these different influences shaped what is important to you?

● Beyond

- Look at the cover art for both *Resurgence* and *Renewal*. How do the covers speak to the concepts of resurgence and renewal?

- What cultural traditions or values have influenced you throughout your life? How have you experienced the intertwining of knowledges or cultures to create something new?

CONNECTING TO COMMUNITY: PROMPTS FOR LEARNING CIRCLES

❭ **Beginning**

- Share your favourite outdoor memory.

- Describe a journey you took, and what you learned along the way.

- Look at the cover artwork for *Renewal*. Describe how you see the art differently after reading about Reanna McKay (Merasty)'s process as an artist and designer.

❭ **Bridging**

- Share a brief story of a time when you felt connected to nature or learned something from the environment.

- Describe a journey you have taken. What did you discover? How did this journey change you or your perspective?

- Share a personal connection to the word *renewal* and any imagery or metaphors you would use to articulate this connection.

● **Beyond**

- Describe a land-based experience that has influenced your worldview, identity, or sense of responsibility to the environment and how it has shaped your thinking about environmental issues or sustainability.

- Share a memorable journey you have taken. Reflect on how this journey has influenced your values, goals, or sense of purpose, and how the lessons learned from this experience continue to shape your decisions or understanding of yourself and the world.

CONNECTING TO LAND-BASED LEARNING

❭ **Beginning**

- Find a comfortable place to observe nature outdoors. What evidence can you find of resurgence or renewal?

- Locate Reanna McKay (Merasty)'s community of Barren Lands First Nation and Reindeer Lake on a map. What can you find out about this community, including the agreements made on the land?

Bridging

- Go outside and choose one natural element to observe closely, such as a cloud, plant, or rock. Look at how it connects to or interacts with other parts of the natural world. Draw a sketch to show these connections, using lines, arrows, and circles to represent how this element relates to its surroundings.

Beyond

- Create a personal map or web of connections to local natural features, marking places that hold significance to you or have impacted your life. Sketch these places or use symbols to represent them.

- Start a new journey by finding a place that connects land and water. This could be within an ecosystem where land and water interact, such as a wetland, or near a structure, such as a footbridge. Spend time listening to and learning from the interactions and encounters you observe in this place. What melding of worldviews do you observe?

CONNECTING TO LAND BACK

- The concepts of resurgence and renewal connect strongly to the idea of Land Back. We live in a time where Western scientific knowledge is finally catching up to traditional Indigenous knowledge. For example, for centuries, many Indigenous communities have practised *cultural burning*—an Indigenous fire-stewardship technique that involves carefully controlled, low-intensity burns to prevent wildfires, manage soil vegetation, prevent overgrowth, and promote ecosystem health.[2] From the time of colonization, these methods were outlawed by authorities who didn't understand the benefits of the practice. However, recent increases in devastating wildfires due to climate change and forest mismanagement have prompted Western science and forestry management agencies to turn to Indigenous knowledges. Studies have shown that cultural

---

2 For more information on the practice of cultural burning, see FireSmart BC, "Cultural Burning & Prescribed Fire," prescribedfire.ca/cultural-burning/, and Parks Canada, "Indigenous Fire Stewardship," parks.canada.ca/nature/science/conservation/feu-fire/autochtones-indigenous.

burning can reduce fuel loads and create fire-resilient landscapes, supporting healthier ecosystems that are more resistant to intense wildfires.[3] Research another example of traditional Indigenous practices being used alongside Western scientific knowledge to promote sustainability.

CONNECTIONS TO OTHER INDIGENOUS RESOURCES

Books

Sometimes I Feel Like a River (Groundwood, 2023; ages 3 and up) and *Sometimes I Feel Like an Oak* (Groundwood, 2024; ages 3–6), by Danielle Daniel. Written by an author of settler and Indigenous ancestry, both books encourage young readers to connect to their feelings in metaphorical ways based on observations of and learning from nature.

Sweetgrass, by Theresa Meuse (Nimbus Publishing, 2022; ages 4–8). This picture book supports learning about the intertwining of the braid of sweetgrass and the significance of this traditional medicine.

The Land We Are: Artists and Writers Unsettle the Politics of Reconciliation, edited by Gabrielle L'Hirondelle Hill and Sophie McCall (Arbeiter Ring Publishing, 2015). This text provides photographs from artists who engage Indigenous knowledges and connections to land through art in a variety of places. They show how to use various materials to convey their activism and learning from land.

---

3   See, for example, Kira M. Hoffman et al., "Conservation of Earth's Biodiversity Is Embedded in Indigenous Fire Stewardship," *Proceedings of the National Academy of Sciences* 118, no. 32, doi.org/10.1073/pnas.2105073118.

Online

"Braiding Ways of Knowing," Reconciling Ways of Knowing, September 24, 2020. <rwok.ca/dialogue3>.
Features a conversation between ecologist and writer Robin Wall Kimmerer and ethnobotanist Dr. Nancy Turner about bringing together Indigenous and Western scientific knowledges and building better relationships across ways of knowing.

"Leanne Betasamosake Simpson: 'f(l)ight' (Album Stream)," by Sarah Murphy, *Exclaim*, September 22, 2016. <exclaim.ca/music/article/leanne_betasamosake _simpson-f_l_ight_album_stream>.
This website includes audio files of Leanne Betasamosake Simpson's music, which would be a great accompaniment to a walk or experience on the land to explore the intertwining of multiple literacies.

National Centre for Collaboration in Indigenous Education. <www.nccie.ca/>.
This website offers a variety of resources, including videos highlighting youth and Elders' voices, digital forums on topics related to intertwining knowledge systems and land-based learning, and snapshots of school community initiatives.

WISE (Wildlife, Indigenous Science, Ecology) Lab. <www.wiselab.ca/research-home>.
This website highlights the work of the WISE Lab, providing examples of using frameworks that weave together Indigenous and Western ways of knowing in environmental and ecological sciences.

"Etuaptmumk: Two-Eyed Seeing | Rebecca Thomas | TEDxNSCCwaterfront," TEDx Talks. <www.youtube.com/watch?v=bA9EwcFbVfg&t=501s>.
In this short video, Rebecca Thomas speaks about her Mi'kmaw perspective and the gift of being able to see through multiple worldviews, building on Two-Eyed Seeing. She concludes with a poem that could support students in voicing their own interpretation of the concepts in spoken words.

THE
FOOTBRIDGE
SERIES

)) ◗ ● ●

T HIS FOOTBRIDGE is built through collaboration. The idea for the Footbridge series came from the inspiring and creative writer Garry Thomas
Morse. He envisioned the first volume, *Resurgence*, and supported connections to many of the contributors in that book. In 2019, Garry shared that
his initial inspiration for the series was the Hagwilget footbridge located
on a First Nations reserve community of the Wet'suwet'en people near
Hazelton, British Columbia. This powerful image from the late 1800s shows
a carefully engineered footbridge that continues to guide us in our work.

(Image A-06048 courtesy of the BC Archives.)